Camping's Forgotten Skills

Backwoods Tips from a Boundary Waters Guide

by Cliff Jacobson

• • •

ICS BOOKS, Inc.
Merrillville, Indiana

Dedication

This book is dedicated to the gallant men and women who donate their time to the Scouting movement. I earned the Eagle badge in 1956 and I continue to cherish the award.

Old time Scouters will smile when they see still practical tips in this book which hail from my Boy Scout days in Illinois and Indiana. Like me, you continue to believe that skills are more important than things!

10 9 8 7 6 5 4 3 2 1

Printed in U.S.A.

Published by:
ICS Books, Inc.
1370 E. 86th Place
Merrillville, IN 46410
800-541-7323

Library of Congress Cataloging-in-Publication Data

Jacobson, Cliff.
    Camping's forgotten skills: backwoods tips from a boundary waters guide Jacobson: illustration by Cliff Moen.
      p. cm.
    Includes index.
    ISBN 0-934802-79-3 $9.99
    1. Wilderness survival. 2. Camping. I. Title
GV200.5.J33   1993
796.54–dc20   92-47409
                     CIP

A Note to the Reader

For most people, canoeing or hiking a deeply remote region is a once-in-a-lifetime experience—one which frequently calls into play superior skills and equipment. As trip length and distance from humankind increase, the window of error narrows, and there are few second chances. Add cold rain and high winds, a grueling route and ambitious schedule, and dangers escalate logarithmically. It is here, beyond the beaten path that you need in-depth knowledge of the outdoors and fail-proof equipment. Canoe an arctic river, hike beyond marked trails, snow camp at 30 below, and you'll want the cutting edge of practiced skills and efficient gear. In *The Forgotten Skills*, we go beyond conventional ways to reflect on obscure but useful skills that you need for a long stay in untamed wilderness.

I think you'll find that some of the methods suggested within these pages—especially those by the guest authors— are truly enlightening, even if you have considerable outdoor experience. Others, like tin can art and jack-knife projects simply add to the fun of camping out.

May you experience light winds, brief rains and bugless days on all your trips. And may you gain knowledge, humility and enthusiasm for the great outdoors and experience the tranquil peace of self-fulfillment from every new adventure.

Cliff Jacobson
1992

Table of Contents

CHAPTER

one

• • •

Fire Making—the Most Forgotten Skill

If there's one skill that establishes expertise in the outdoors, it is the ability to make a cheery campfire in any weather. In theory, the procedure is simple; in practice it is beyond the ability of most people who use the backcountry. Consider this:

In a class called "The Forgotten Skills", which I teach for the Science Museum of Minnesota, students are given one hour to collect dry wood, prepare tinder and kindling, and ignite a blaze that will bring a quart of water to a boil. Everyone receives two matches and is allowed to use an axe, folding saw, and knife. No liquid fuel, paper, birch bark, dry leaves or grasses are allowed.

Experienced outdoors people usually begin by sawing a chunk of log off a dead, downed tree. Then they split the piece and slice the dry heartwood into match thin shavings (tinder). When they've produced a handful of shavings, they gather them into a loose pile and strike their match. As the blaze grows, they add thin splittings, one at a time, until the fire takes hold. If dry fuel is at hand, and the weather cooperates, they'll bask in the warmth of their accomplishment in less than five minutes.

Those less practiced in the art of fire making begin differently. Invariably, they pick small dead twigs off the nearest tree and methodically arrange them into a low tipi. Then they apply their match to the criss-crossed wood and hope for the best. If the fuel is dry, the procedure usually works. If not, there's a muffled fizzle and they begin anew, oblivious to the fact that this is their last match, and what failed once will fail again. One fourth of the students will use both their matches and fail to start a fire under text book perfect conditions, regardless of how many matches they use. And if the day deteriorates to persistent rain, barely one in ten will produce a reliable blaze.

If you've ever watched an experienced outdoorsperson make fire on a rainy day, you'll find the presence of these variables:

1. Tinder is thin, no thicker than a match. Trying to ignite sticks thicker than this is an exercise in futility, even when they are dry. Almost without exception, beginners choose tinder which is too thick.

2. Non-use of paper or liquid fuel even when they are available. Paper is "hydrophyllic": it absorbs moisture from the air and is useless in damp weather. If you've ever left a newspaper outside overnight, you know the phenomenon. Liquid fuel is dangerous; it marks you as a novice, and it provides only a few seconds of heat—seldom enough to start a badly built fire. Besides, liquid fuel is a precious commodity in the backcountry; a wasted splash on wet wood might be enough to fuel your stove for an hour!

3. Non-use of tipis, log cabins, leantos, and other exotic fire lays. An overburden of wood draws heat from a developing flame—exactly what you don't want in inclement weather. One of the best ways to learn about fire building is to watch a primitive fire

making demonstration. Here, the builder must capture heat from a single spark (or glowing coal) and gently nurse it to flame. This is accomplished by first adding fine tinder, then the thinnest of sticks, one at a time, to the nucleus of the young flame. The fire is never transferred to a pre-fab structure of any kind. Like a fine home, it is carefuly erected one stick at a time.

4. The fire almost always starts with one match. Like a good hunter, who shoots only when sure of his or her target, the experienced fire-maker strikes the match only when certain of success.

5. An almost complete absence of smoke, even if the wood is damp. Rationale? Cut kindling thin enough, and it will burn completely. And provide plenty of air space between sticks. Smoke is nature's way of saying "you're smothering the flames!"

FIRE MAKING TOOLS

A knife, axe, and saw are essential tools on a rainy day. Simply saw dead logs into foot long lengths and split them with the axe to get at the dry heartwood inside. A full size axe will produce a shedful of splittings in record time, but a handaxe makes a fine splitting wedge if you lightly set the blade into the end grain of a log section and hold the handle tight while a friend pounds the head through with a chunk of log. From here, it's simply a matter of splitting the splittings into finer and finer pieces until you have readily burnable material which is "no thicker than a match".

TRICKS

Fuzz Stick Here's a useful "forgotton skill" which old scoutmasters will recognize. Simply frizz up two or three thumb-thick softwood sticks and arrange them tipi style, as illustrated in figure 1-1. Strike your match beneath, and in seconds you'll have a cheery blaze. Carve several fuzz sticks ahead of time and keep them in a plastic bag for emergencies.

Some campers have difficulty cutting long, thin shavings or a fuzz stick. Figures 1-2 and 1-3 show two reliable methods. The "sawing" motion illustrated in figure 1-2 works best with a small, thin-bladed knife. Even a tiny pen knife (or nail file!) will produce long, thin shavings when used this way. If you have a thick-bladed, powerful knife, the "reverse hand" procedure will slice a handful of shavings in seconds.

Conifer Resins Resins from the southern pines and western conifers are extremely volatile. So too are those from the northern spruce and balsam fir. In summer, the balsam fir produces quarter size blisters on its bark, which are easily pierced with a sharp stick. The liquid pitch is as volatile as kerosine. In western forests, seek out the remains of an old, fallen Douglas fir. Search the brownish, crumbly debris for solid pieces of wood which are streaked with resin. Use this "fat wood" to start your fire. On the prairies of the midwest, collect the dead branches of cottonwood trees. In the desert, dry mesquite is the best kindling you'll find.

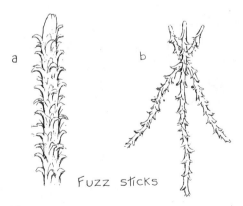

Figure 1-1

Saw rapidly to
produce long,
thin shavings

Figure 1-2

Stumps and Roots   Trees concentrate volatile resins in their roots, so a dry stump is a rare find. Conifers, especially, are so rich in pitch that they will burn on their own for hours—the reason why fires in evergreen forests are so devastating.

Standing Wood from Clearings   Bacteria and fungi prefer cool, shady places, so the dead, standing wood in sun-lit clearings is less likely to be rotten than that gathered from deep within the forest. For this reason, you should seek out open areas and wood that does not touch the ground.

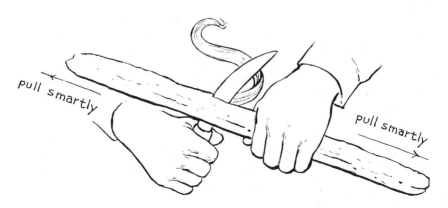

Pull smartly

Pull smartly

Figure 1-3

Caution: dry wood piles in deserts and rain forests provide homes for all matter of stinging critters. In the southwest, the danger is scorpions; in the west, it's biting ants. And in lake country of the far north, there are mice, beetles and worms. It follows that dead wood should be piled well away from tents.

Bark With the exception of birch bark and a few others which burn with ferocity, bark rates poorly as fire-starting material. Fact is, bark is primarly a protective material, and as such, is designed to prevent the tree from burning in a severe fire. The giant redwoods owe their longevity largely to their thick, fire-resistant bark, which may be a foot thick!

Draft A fire needs plenty of well-directed air to burn cleanly. You can provide a "chimney" of sorts by always adding two similarly sized pieces of wood to the flames at a time. Each splitting should be placed parallel to the other—and the distance between them should be no greater than the diameter of the largest piece. Air needs an entry and exit way: fires burn best if opposite sides of the fire base are left open to the air.

To "bank" your fire for slower burning, simply top your fire with a wide bank of closely spaced parallel sticks (bark on).

Fire-Starters A candle stub, flattened cardboard milk carton, and/or tube of liquid fire-starting gel can be a lifesaver under certain conditions. Inexpensive fire-starters are easily made by soaking cotton cloth, commercial lamp wicking, or newspaper in melted paraffin. When the wax has set, cut the cloth or paper into short strips and use these to start your fire. Caution: Paraffin has a very low flash point and may burst into flame if you heat it directly on a stove burner. A "double-boiler" eliminates most danger. Cotton balls dipped in Vaseline also make handy fire-starters on a rainy day.

Maintaining a Campfire on Snow You must provide a platform for your fire or it will sink into the snow and go out. A base of parallel logs works fine. Some snow campers carry an aluminum pizza pan or cookie sheet for this purpose. The pan must be insulated from the snow with logs or branches.

MAKING FIRE BY FRICTION

Except for fun, and an unusual survival situation, I can't think of any reason why you would want to make a fire-by-friction. Nonetheless, the ability to make fire-by-friction marks you as a pro and will attract glowing admiration by onlookers. Here's the time-proven way to make fire by "rubbing sticks together".

You'll need these materials: *Drill (spindle):* made from a dry, seasoned piece of soft, non-resinous wood, the spindle should be about five-eighths inch thick, and 8-10 inches long, or about half the length of your shin bone. Soft "hardwoods" like cottonwood, quaking aspen (popple), red and white cedar, balsa, willow, elm, Arizona yucca and bald cypress make the best fire sets. Wood obtained from the roots (especially, elm, willow and cottonwood) is often better than that from limbs and trunks.

Fire Board Make the fire board or "hearth" from the same wood or a slightly softer wood than the spindle. It should be one-half to three-eighths of an inch thick. The idea is to spin the drill fast enough to create fine, charred dust at the point. When the dust reaches critical temperature, it begins to smoke, hopefully producing a tiny ember which must be nursed to flame. Selection of wood for fire board and spindle is critical: not all combinations of woods will produce enough heat to cause combustion.

When I was a boy scout, I routinely made fires by friction from gathered materials, disdaining the commercial

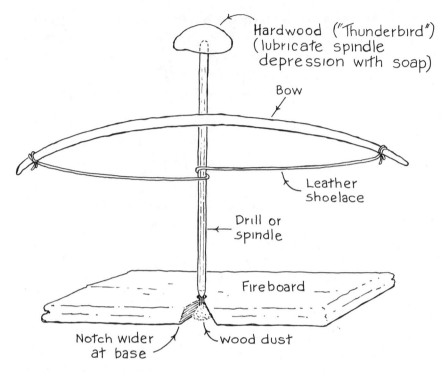

Figure 1-4

kits which could be purchased from scout headquarters. I learned that a dry, dead branch makes the best spindle, while a split log makes a good fire board.

Palm Socket or "Thunderbird" A hardwood block with a half-inch deep hole in it to secure the drill top. Suggestion: place some boot grease or Vaseline in the hollow to lubricate the spindle top.

The "bow" can be made from any branch and should be about two feet long. A rawhide shoe lace makes a better "thong" than a nylon one, which may have to be "roughed up" (draw it back and forth several times over a rough rock) to provide good purchase on the spindle.

Tinder is traditionally made from the dry, fibrous bark of the red or white cedar, or from the inner bark of the cottonwood or elm. Gather a handful of bark and pound it to a pulp with a heavy, blunt stick. Then, roll the bark between your hands and tease it to a fluffy, cotton-like ball. Disregard any granular particles in the bark. Other favored tinders include cattail and milkweed down, bird down and the silky tops of goldenrod and other flowers. Unravelled, pounded strands of untreated sisal and hemp rope occasionally make acceptable tinder. Charred cloth—like that required for making fire by "flint and steel" (see following section)—works great.

PREPARING THE FIRE BOARD

With the point of your knife, whittle a deep gouge three-fourths of an inch from the edge of the fire board, then assemble the bow, drill, and palm piece, and draw the bow rapidly back and forth to drive the spindle about one-eighth inch into the hearth. Your hearth should now have a blackened socket that is equal to the diameter of the drill. Next, cut a narrow, U-shaped notch from the edge of the fire board almost to the center of the gouge. Taper the notch so it is wider on the bottom than the top.

TO MAKE FIRE

Now, you're ready to make fire. Flatten some tinder and place it under the notch of the fire board. Assemble the drill kit and and bear down solidly on the palm piece as you stroke back and forth with the bow. Soon, smoke will arise from the fire board and a dark brownish black powder will begin to accumulate in the notch below. Keep pressure on the palm piece and keep sawing until the notch is almost full of the black powder. When the smoke coming from the fire board is almost too thick to bear, lift the hearth and tinder and blow gently on the ember—or fan the fire board up and down with your hands to increase air flow. If the tinder bursts into fire, you've done everything right.

It's unlikely you'll succeed in your first fire-by-friction attempt. But patience has its own rewards, and you'll burn plenty of calories as you saw away. Check the tinder and notch in the fire-board before you try again: if necessary replace partially burned tinder and whittle a new notch. The world record for making fire-by-friction at a Boy Scout camporee is six seconds! Practiced South American natives and Australian bush men can probably do it faster than that.·

REASONS WHY FIRE-BY-FRICTION FIRES DON'T START:

1. The notch in the fire-board is the wrong size. You'll have to experiment.
2. Slippage between spindle and cord reduces friction. Solution: re-adjust the cord, roughen spindle sides, lubricate the palm piece.
3. Tinder isn't dry enough or fine enough.
4. Woods are not completely dry or seasoned, or you've used the wrong kind.

FIRE BY FLINT-AND-STEEL

This procedure is simple, fast, and draws considerable envy from the crowd. I have a friend who belongs to a primitive weapons (mountain man) brigade, which disallows the use of matches. He routinely makes fire by flint-and-steel faster than most folks can strike a match. Making fire by flint-and-steel is easy: beginners can usually succeed after a few attempts if they have the right tinder and tools.

You'll need a chunk of flint, a piece of steel, and some well-charred cotton or linen cloth. Unpolished flint, quartz, or chert picked from the forest floor will do, but why mess around when you can buy good quality gun flints for less than a dollar at any gun shop that sells muzzle-loading equipment. A large, "musket" flint is easier to handle than a small rifle or pistol flint.

Theoretically, pounded bark, like that used to make fire-by-friction, will ignite by flint-and-steel. Perhaps, but I've been unsuccessful with every type of tinder except charred cloth and fine steel wool. The cloth must be pure cotton or linen. To char the fabric, ignite it and immediately drop it into a small metal can. Snap on the can cover and allow the flaming material to completely smolder and blacken. I've found that the material will char more uniformly if there is a small pin-hole in the lid of the can.

Steels   Many modern knife steels—especially stainless—are unsuitable for making fire by flint-and-steel. A high carbon steel pocket or butcher knife, or an old file, usually works fine. You'll have to experiment. Or, for a few dollars, you can buy a traditional eighteenth century "fire steel" which is correctly tempered and designed to eliminate bruised knuckles. Note: some foreign made fire-steels are tempered wrong and won't produce sparks. Hand forged, high-carbon American made steels generally work best. Any blacksmith can make a fire-steel for you by duplicating figure 1-5.

Using Flint and Steel Together   Place a wad of native tinder—pulverized bark, cattail down, whisker thin softwood shavings, etc.—on the ground and put a quarter sized piece of charred cloth on top of the tinder. Strike the flint sharply against the fire-steel or file to send a shower of sparks into the charred cloth. Some people prefer to hold the flint in one hand and strike blows with the steel. You'll have to experiment. A trapped spark will begin to glow immediately and burn a hole in the charred cloth.

Now, act quickly. Gently cup the tinder around the charred cloth and blow the mass into flames. Add more tinder, then kindling, and soon you'll have a cheery blaze. Once you get on to it, you can make fire by this method in less than a minute.

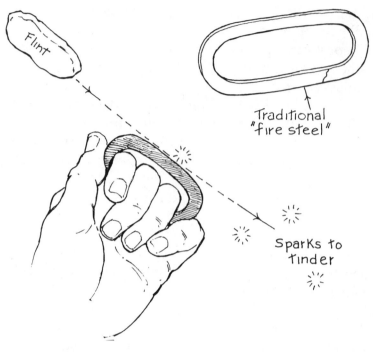

Figure 1-5

METAL MATCH

A composite metal rod which produces a shower of very hot sparks when scraped quickly with a knife blade. "Metal matches" are available at every camping shop. They have an unlimited shelf life and so are true survival tools. They produce sparks which are much hotter than those obtainable with flint-and-steel, and can easily ignite stubborn tinder. Simply scrape small filings into a pile with the edge of your pocket knife, then ignite the mass with sparks from the metal match. Simple as pie.

FIRE SAW

Here's a primitive method which is surprisingly easy to use. Simply split a piece of bamboo down the center then cut a notch at right angles through one of the split sections, as

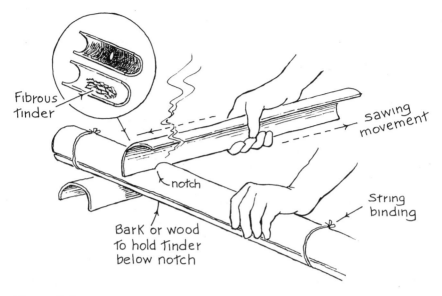

Fibrous Tinder

sawing movement

notch

String binding

Bark or wood To hold tinder below notch

Figure 1-6

illustrated in figure 1-6. Place a thick wad of tinder (best is fiber scraped from a piece of bamboo) in the concave section of the splitting, beneath the notch. Loosely secure the tinder by placing bark or dry leaves beneath it.

Set this fire base firmly against a rock or log and place a long edge of your "saw" (the other bamboo splitting) into the notch. Rapidly saw the bamboo piece back and forth until you get heavy smoke and an ember. Then, nurse the ember to flame as explained in making "fire-by-friction". Note the similarity between the bow/drill and bamboo saw methods of making fire. Both procedures create an ember by heat of friction: one uses a spinning drill, the other a sawing action. Try them both and decide for yourself which is superior.

MAKING FIRE WITH FIREARMS

In the days of black powder and flintlock rifles, it was easy to make fire. Just plug the flash hole in the barrel with a sliver of wood, prime the pan with powder and set the lock against flammable tinder, then pull the trigger. Modern guns are no match for the fire-making utility of flintlocks, but they can improve your odds of producing fire in damp weather if you extract the gun powder and use it to prime your tinder.

To remove the powder from a shotgun shell, simply cut the brass base off the plastic shell casing with your pocket knife. If you have a rifle, use a pliers to extract the bullet. Or, nose the bullet lightly into the muzzle and wiggle the cartridge case back and forth until the bullet is free.

Contrary to popular belief, modern nitrocellulose powders are not at all easy to ignite. A light spark, like that produced from a "flint-and-steel" kit, usually isn't enough. Often, you need a good, hot flame. A match will work, as will a shower of sparks scraped from a "metal match". Some old time handbooks suggest you extract the bullet and half the powder, then replace the bullet with a light cloth wad to hold the powder in place. You are then told to fire the gun into a depression filled with gun powder which you have extracted from several shells. The powder is supposed to ignite at the shot. Instead, it will probably be blown all over the country side by the force of the escaping gases. It's doubtful any will catch fire.

Another equally questionable method suggests that you empty four-fifths of the gun powder in a rifle or shotgun shell into a small piece of cotton cloth, which is then wadded up and loosely loaded into the muzzle of the gun. Then you fire the cartridge (with bullet and four-fifths of the powder removed) into the air. The cloth should catch fire and return to the ground smoldering, which it may if the cartridge is loaded with black powder—a propellent no longer used in breech-loading firearms. Fact is, the procedure almost never works with modern guns and modern powders.

Because I value my guns, I would never utilize either method. Even if these procedures work, they are apt to clog or damage the barrel. The super light load might not generate enough pressure to seal the cartridge case in the breech, the result of which may be dangerous gas leakage around the bolt. Seems to me that if you have sense enough to carry a firearm afield, you'll have sense enough to carry proper fire making equipment as well!

Nonetheless, if you absolutely must start a fire with a modern firearm, the following method, suggested by Mike Dawson on page 59 of the January, 1990 issue of *The American Rifleman Magazine*, usually works.

1. Empty the powder charge from a *center-fire* rifle or handgun into the center of a cotton bandana, then chamber the empty, primed case into the weapon.
2. Set the muzzle on the powder pile and wrap the corners of the cloth around the barrel.
3. Fire the weapon. Primer flame will shoot out of the muzzle and ignite the powder and cloth.

In his experiments, Dawson noted that firing an empty, primed (no powder) case directly into a pile of loose smokeless powder usually scattered, but did not ignite, the powder.

AUTOMOBILE BATTERIES, CIGAR LIGHTERS AND ROAD FLARES

An automobile battery can be used to make fire if you have jumper cables. Simply hook up the cables and quickly slap the wires together. A substantial spark—which may be used to ignite tinder, gun powder, a liquid fuel soaked rag, etc.—will result.

Caution: Automobile batteries produce hydrogen gas which, when combined with oxygen, is very explosive. If a hot spark lands on your battery...BOOM! For this reason, you should protect the battery from sparks and be well away from it when you slap the cables together.

The cigar lighter in your car provides ready ignition for flammable materials, as does a spark plug wire. Simply unclip the plug wire from a running engine and place it a short distance from the spark plug. A long hot spark will develop at firing intervals. A liquid fuel-soaked rag, wrapped around a stick (makes a convenient torch) can be used to catch the spark. Tip: your torch will burn longer if you mix some crank-case oil with the liquid fuel. Highway flares too, make excellent fire starters and are easily ignited in any weather.

FIRE BY MAGNIFYING GLASS

Every old camping book has a section on how to make fire with a magnifying glass. You are told to simply pinpoint the light on dry tinder and in seconds there'll be fire. Don't you believe it! Every kid has played with magnifying glasses enough to know that where there's smoke, there's seldom fire. But the procedure will work, if you have a reasonably large lens. For best results, the magnifier should be at least two inches in diameter. A smaller glass will work, but only in the brightest sunlight with superb tinder, or with tinder that has been primed with liquid fuel.

COOKING FIRES

The Modified Key-Hole   Some years ago, while on a canoe trip in northern Canada, one of my two liquid fuel stoves failed while preparing the evening meal. Much as I love campfires, I'm not much for cooking on them, so I delegated the responsibility to a young man who had spent considerable time canoeing in Quetico Provincial Park.

As I worked over the one remaining stove, I watched the young man organize our hastily built warming fire into a precision cooking tool. First, he built a long, stone trench at one end, carefully adjusting the rocks so that they would support our two largest cooking pots. Then he propped rocks at the back of the fire place to draw smoke away from the cooking (trench) end. Last step was to scrape coals and

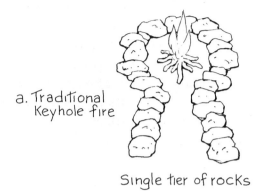

a. Traditional
   Keyhole fire

Single tier of rocks

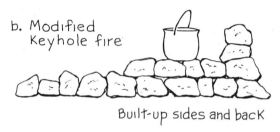

b. Modified
   Keyhole fire

Built-up sides and back

Figure 1-7

burning material into the trench, the temperature of which was regulated by adding or deleting embers. He called his design a "reflector trench", though in its purest form, it would be called a "key hole".

Outdoors handbooks define dozens of fire styles, though the "modified" key-hole illustrated in figure 1-7 outperfoms them all. The modified version beats the traditional style for cooking and warming. Here's why:

1. The large "key-hole" opening radiates warmth a full 360 degrees, while the "back-rock" reflector draws smoke away from the cook and concentrates heat into the trench.

2. The narrow trench provides a rock-stable pot support.

3.   Heat can be adjusted in two ways: by scraping more or less coals into the trench, or by increasing or decreasing the area of the back-rock damper. Remove the back-rock for rapid, flow-through ventilation, or build it high to dampen air movement for slower cooking. In high winds, construct rock wings on each side of the reflector to produce a three-sided chimney that will keep smoke from swirling into the face of the cook.

CONSTRUCTION TIPS

Eighteen inches in diameter is a good size for the warming section of a key-hole fire. Taper the trench, as illustrated, so it will support your widest and narrowest pots. Build one or two steps into the trench side-walls so you can move pots to higher or lower temperature levels, as necessary.

LEAVE NO TRACE FIRES

The modified key-hole fire has its place, which is in organized camps and the deepest of wilderness. Everywhere else, "leave no trace" fires are the rule, not the exception. Here are the recommended procedures for building them.

Fire Pans   This is the most acceptable method of fire maintenance. Sometimes it is not practical to carry a heavy fire pan and you must consider other methods.

On Sod or Sand   Cut a circle in the grass equal to the size of your fire and carefully remove and invert the sod cap. Place the inverted sod cap on the grass nearby, then dig an eight inch deep hole and pile the dirt on top of the sod. Build your fire in the hole and feed the flames with small sticks that will burn quickly. The idea is to leave ashes, not charred wood behind. When the blaze has almost completely extinguished itself, drown the coals with water, if available. Otherwise, smother them with tightly packed soil. Then, replace the sod cap and smooth the surrounding terrain. With care, there should be absolutely no trace of fire remains.

This method takes only a few minutes and works so well it has been recommended by the Minnesota Department of Natural Resources. Over the last 20 years, students in my eighth grade environmental science class have used it exclusively to build more than 500 fires around the perimeter of our school's athletic field. The kids clean up so perfectly that not even I can find a trace of their fire sites.

This practice is discouraged in some areas because it tends to ruin root systems. Consult your local Department of Natural Resources agency or Park Service for acceptable fire maintenance in the area you will camp.

On Rock Burn every last stick of wood and drown the ashes with water. Then, scatter the rocks and smooth the area to a natural look. Except for black carbon deposits on the fireplace rocks, there should be no trace of a blaze. If fire-blackened rocks are a concern—and they are in frequently used wilderness areas—you'll want to completely contain your fire in an iron "fire pan", which is designed for this purpose. "Fire pans" are available from many western outfitters or you can easily make your own. One camper I know uses an inverted galvanized garbage can lid! The lid wears through in a season or two but it's lightweight and inexpensive.

Tip: use a plastic bag as a glove to prevent charcoal-blackened hands when you clean up fire remains.

Here's another tip which works surprisingly well: Old timers know that if you coat pot bottoms with liquid soap before placing them on the fire, the soot will wash off easily. Ditto for rocks! If you use this procedure, please wash off the soap well away (100 feet is recommended) from a water source, or scatter the rocks on high ground and let rain do the rest.

FIRE ACCESSORIES

Fire Irons If you've ever had a kettle drown your fire when the log on which it was sitting burned through, you'll appreciate an unburnable pot support of some kind. A grill solves the problem but leaves you with a carbon-coated mess which is awkward to pack and difficult to clean. For this reason, old timers generally preferred to use a pair of iron rods to support their cookware. "Fire irons", as they are called, are difficult to find these days, though any blacksmith can make them for you in a few minutes. Forged irons rods are traditional, but austere steel angle works as well. Make your fire irons about two feet long so they'll bridge a wide blaze.

Tip: *you'll be able to cook more hamburgers on your grill if you support it with fire irons instead of logs.*

Tongs A steel pliers, worn in an aging leather belt sheath, is the traditional fire place tongs and fix everything tool. However, for strictly fire use, the "official" Boy Scout aluminum pliers/pot lifter is much lighter and handier. Mine is 10 years old now and still going strong.

Tripods   A tripod was standard equipment for every turn-of-the-century cooking fire. And for good reason. It takes time to fashion a sturdy rock support for the coffee pot. But with three sticks and a length of twine, you'll have the kettle "bi'ling" in minutes.

A tripod makes even more sense if you cook on a modified key hole fire. Erect the tripod over the open key hole and build up the flames. Suspend your coffee pot from the tripod on a metal S-hook or Y-branch and keep up the heat here while you sauté delicate foods on low level coals in the narrow trench.

Tip: *if you tie two hooks—one high, one low—on the rope suspended from your tripod, you can easily move the kettle to higher or lower heat, as the need arises. When using the high hook, sling the dangling length of rope over the tripod top so it won't burn through. Or substitute light chain for rope and forget this foolishness. In chapter 3, you'll discover a slick way to cook fresh caught fish (no pots or pans needed!) on your tripod!*

two

• • •

The Basic Cook Kit

Commercial cook sets are like drugstore first-aid kits; you get just enough to survive the day, but not enough to comfortably enjoy it. So if your idea of backwoods cooking is one pot boiling-glop, read no further. This equipment is for those who relish good food and are willing to take the time to prepare it.

Don't misinterpret: you don't need to slave for hours over simmering coals to produce fine meals. As you'll discover in the next chapter, the right tools, an enlightened attitude, and 30 minutes will do it.

HARDWARE

Before 1950, heavy cast iron skillets and dutch ovens were the cookware of the day. And for good reason: the thick, black metal distributes heat evenly on high flames or smoldering embers, something which can't be said for modern materials. When it comes to cooking over fire, cast iron rates number one. Then comes heavy cast aluminum, well-seasoned (more on this later) carbon steel, copper-clad stainless steel, and stamped aluminum. Experienced campers know that stamped aluminum and non-copper-coated stainless steel pans burn everything, but in keeping with tradition, they refuse to divulge this information to anyone.

For example, in 1951, I purchased a solo cook-kit which had a paper thin aluminum skillet, quart pot with cover, and a deep plate that doubled as a pan lid. An attractive little unit, it looked woodsy and weighed under a pound, but everything I cooked in it stuck firmly to the bottom. After using a sharp-edged spoon and two Brillo™ pads to chisel out the blackened remains of my first pancake, I quietly relegated the outfit to the attic.

Aluminum cook kits like the one I've described are still popular, even though they are awful. Nonetheless, every new camper acquires one, often, as a ceremonial hand-me-down from an old timer who wants a good home for his first mistake.

To fix fine foods you'll need sturdy pots and pans which cook evenly. You can get very good camp sets, but these are expensive and often contain components you don't need. I buy only the smaller nesting pots at outdoor stores and assemble the skillets, coffee pot and cooking utensils from reliable, local materials. You'll find that what works well at home will, with some simple modifications, do wonders afield. For a party of four, you'll need:

Three nesting pots with covers, the largest of which should hold 16 cups so you can cook pasta without gluing it to the bottom. Pots may be stainless steel, aluminum, or porcelain-lined carbon steel. I've used them all and prefer copper-clad stainless if I can get it. But, have you priced these pots lately?

HOW TO DETERMINE THE
SIZE OF YOUR LARGEST POT

As a rule, your largest pot should allow a 2-1/2 cup serving per person, plus two additional "cups for the pot" so you can stir without slopping over the sides. Thus, a 12 cup pot is about right for four, 14-1/2 cups for five, etc.

Fill the space inside your smallest pot with nesting bowls, cups or dish washing materials. It won't take you long to discover that a bulky coffee pot or tea kettle fouls up the whole packing system. For this reason, I always pack my tea kettle separately or, if space and weight is a concern, I don't bring it at all.

POT HANDLES

Best are wide bail handles that lock upright and flip neatly out of the way when not in use. Engineering like this costs money, so if price is a concern, build your kit from conventional discount store cook ware.

Last year, I bought a 40 cup porcelain-lined steel pot for use when I guide large groups. It has a welded handle on each side, but no bail. Most of the time I cook on a stove so this set up is perfectly adequate. When I do use a fire, I just set the pot on a custom-built stainless steel grate and handle it with a pair of bandanas. At first, I thought I'd miss the handy bailer. But the "ears" work fine. The inexpensive porcelain kettle resists burns and it cleans more easily than aluminum or stainless.

Tip: *carry fresh onions, green peppers and other crushables inside your tea kettle. Separate vegetables by type and store them in dry cotton sacks.*

SKILLETS

If there's such a thing as a good lightweight camp skillet, I haven't found it! For years I relied on a well-seasoned carbon steel pan for all my cooking, and this is still a good choice.[1] But it's an ongoing process to keep carbon

[1]Here's how to season a new carbon steel pan or cast iron skillet. Coat the pan (inside and out) with high temperature peanut oil, then place it in a 350° oven for two hours. This completes the initial seasoning process. To clean the skillet: wipe out food remains with paper toweling, then boil out stubborn food particles with water, if necessary. Never use detergent on a seasoned steel skillet! Dry the pan and rub in more oil. An occasional coating of peanut oil or Pam™ keeps pans seasoned and rust-free. Aluminum and stainless steel skillets need no seasoning but will benefit by occasional applications of oil.

steel rust free. So now I buy the best Teflon-coated aluminum skillet available, then I remove the fixed plastic handle and install a quickly removeable spring wire handle which I bend from 0.187 inch diameter spring steel.

The mounting bracket for the handle is made from hardware store aluminum flat stock. It secures with two small brass bolts which are easily removed when the pan wears out.

Tip: *install a universal mounting bracket on all your pots so you can snap on a bayonet handle for easier pouring.*

One 10 inch diameter Teflon skillet is adequate for a party of four. For larger groups, a 12 inch pan is better. When the crew size climbs above eight, I carry two skillets.

BLACKENED POTS COOK BEST!

Everyone knows that black absorbs more heat than silver, so why do makers of cookware insist on bright, polished finishes? You can let time and smoky fires blacken your pot bottoms, but the carbon residue will contaminate everything it touches. If you use this procedure, place each pot in a separate cotton sack before you pack your kit.

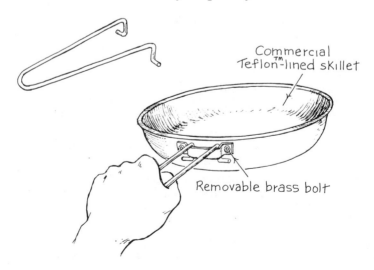

Commercial
Teflon™-lined skillet

Removable brass bolt

Figure 2-1

Cookware may also be darkened chemically with "Alu-ma-black"—a chemical developed for blackening aluminum gun sights and mounts, or gun blue, which turns carbon steel blue-black. You can get these products at any gun shop. I don't know any chemicals which work on stainless steel.

COVERS

You should have a tight-fitting cover for every pot and pan you own. A skillet that substitutes as a pot cover is adequate only when you don't need to fry and boil at the same time. Each cover should have a metal D-ring or bracket so you can remove it with a knife tip or fork.

When you're cooking above the tree line, or for large parties, a cover and an insulated cozy can be a life-saver. Consider this scenario:

It's 36 degrees and the wind is howling bloody murder. You place 18 cups of cold water into your largest pot, dump in the Red River cereal, and turn your stove to high. The intense localized heat of the flame suggests you'd better stir constantly to prevent burning. Twenty minutes pass before the porridge begins to boil. Even with a makeshift wind-screen, enough cold air reaches the pot to prevent efficient cooking. What to do?

Shut off the stove and remove the cereal. Snap on a cover and set the hot pot on a closed cell foam pad. Now, pile some loose clothing over the pot and go watch the sun rise for 15 minutes while your "slow cooker" does its thing. The makeshift "tea cozy" saves liquid fuel and the displeasure of cleaning burned food off the bottom of your pot.

For the ultimate in thermal efficiency, make insulated fabric "cozies" for all your pots and use them while your stove is running. I construct my cozies from two pieces of Thinsulate™ filled material. One part slips over the metal cover and has a long skirt which drapes three-fourths the way down the pot sides. This permits running the stove full blast without burning the hem of the cozy. A second, insulated band Velcroes™ around the pot and covers the remaining naked metal when the stove is shut off.

Rick Garza, a backpacker/canoeist and scoutmaster from Houston, Texas suggests an even more efficient solution. Rick glues closed cell foam to the pot sides and covers, then he fiberglasses over the foam. Black, heat-resistant paint is then applied to the fiberglass. The insulation stays put and the fiberglass protected foam won't burn if flame inadvertently touches it.

On a recent 16 day trip down the Hood River, north of the Arctic circle, I used cozies and foam to insulate my pots while cooking for a crew of 10. Breakfasts and suppers were prepared on three stoves—two Optimus 111B's and an MSR XGK. I frequently made popcorn, boiled tea and dish water and otherwise made no effort to conserve stove fuel. Nonetheless, we used barely two gallons of liquid fuel—a 50 percent or more savings over that which I had predicted we would have used with non-insulated pots.

OVENS

There are dutch ovens, reflector ovens, triple-pan and Jello-mold ovens. My book, *The Basic Essentials of Cooking*, details procedures for using all of them. New on the market is the"Bakepacker"—a clever "steam-powered" oven which produces tasty but amorphous bake stuff. Most camping stores have it.

BAMBOO STEAMER

For my birthday, my daughter gave me a bamboo steamer with the reasurring words that I'd like it for camping. She was right: the little steamer is a practical addition to my cook-set. With it, I can rehydrate dried fruit and vegetables much faster and with far less water, than boiling. Top dehydrated apples and apricots with brown sugar and cinnamon, and steam them for five mintues, and you'll have a luscious dessert everyone will enjoy.

To make bread in a bamboo steamer, simply place prepared dough in an open, heat-resistant, plastic bag. The procedure is similar to that of a "Bakepacker" oven. Light steaming will rejuvenate almost stale bagels, pita bread and tortillas. And it's a fast way to prepare great tasting fish. Try steaming fresh caught fish fillets that have been covered with margarine, onion, cheese and garlic.

CUPS, BOWLS, SILVERWARE

I pack a plastic bowl and an insulated cup for each person. A spoon is essential, while a fork is a welcome luxury. Everyone should have their own knife. A zippered fabric bag keeps utensils clean and organized. I also carry two stainless steel Sierra cups for use as ladles.

PROTECTIVE FABRIC POT BAG

A generously sized cotton or nylon bag keeps pots clean and organized. The bag should be "porous" so it won't pool water when pots are put away wet.

FABRIC UTENSIL ROLL

For years, I scoffed at utensil rolls; now I wouldn't be without one. Mine has snaps (ties work as well) at the top so I can hang it from a branch or overhead line. Contents include a large wooden spoon, wire whip, rubber spatula, bamboo tongs, full sized can opener, regulation cast aluminum boy scout pot gripper (these are the best!), and four universal spring steel pan handles like the ones mentioned earlier.

SPICE BAG

No cook set would be complete without a full complement of spices which I carry in a round-bottomed nylon bag.

HEAD LAMP

For years, I relied on a small, high intensity flashlight for all my camping. Then, when I began to lead canoe trips, I migrated to a head lamp because it simplified the preparation of moonlight suppers. Lightweight, AA-battery headlamps are adequate, though I prefer my professional miner's lamp which runs on four D-cells and illuminates the whole world.

CLEANING MATERIALS

I carry a 3M nylon "scratcher", copper sponge, Teflon-safe nylon sponge, and a small bottle of biodegradable detergent. Everything goes in a Zip-lock bag which nests inside a nylon sack. Tip: pine cones make great scouring pads!

That's the line up of things you need for outdoor cooking. For preparing gourmet foods you can add fancy commercial ovens, woks, pressure cookers, stainless steel bowls and plates, and exotic spices. But these things aren't necessary to prepare good food in the wilderness. Sure, you can get by with two nesting billy's and a stamped aluminum skillet. Some parties do. But I question if what they eat is worth the few pounds they save by going second class.

See my book *The Basic Essentials of Cooking in the Outdoors,* for specific recipes and meal preparation procedures using this equipment. Here's a summary of what you need to feed a crew of four:

> One, 12 cup pot and two smaller nesting pots with covers

> Tea kettle: 12–24 cup capacity

A 10 or 12 inch diameter Teflon-coated skillet

Cup, bowl, spoon and fork for everyone

Two stainless steel Sierra cups for use as ladles

Detachable handles that will fit all your cookware

CHAPTER
three
• • •

Beyond Food Basics

A Compendium of Tasty Food Ideas and Preparation Techniques

Seven a.m. and breakfast in the backcountry. On hand, is a dozen eggs and half a loaf of bread, a somewhat pulpy onion, and a fist-sized chunk of cheddar cheese. Hmmm. Why not wow 'em with an onion/cheese omelet and honey/buttered toast?

You rake some coals into the trench of your keyhole fire and set your skillet on to heat. The magic of your culinary talents are about to be unveiled.

OMELETS AND TOAST

Omelets are easy to make if you have a good, even-heating skillet. For semi-permanent camps where weight is no concern, you can't beat seasoned cast iron. Otherwise, my vote goes to Teflon-coated Mirro aluminum. Adjust the stove to

Figure 3-1

low or the fire to simmer, and pre-heat your lightly oiled skillet. I prefer peanut oil for backwoods cooking because of its high temperature stability.

Beat two or three eggs and pour them into the hot pan. Immediately place diced, raw onion and thin slices of cheese on top (a small shredder is useful). Salt and pepper to taste and cover immediately. Continue to fry on low-moderate heat until the surface of the egg becomes glassy. Then, fold the omelet in half, cover and continue cooking for another 30 seconds. Tip: add a tablespoon of water to the hot pan before you fold the omelet. The steam produced will speed cooking and make the omelet more moist.

To toast bread in a skillet, shake some salt onto the surface of a clean, dry (no oil) skillet, and set the bread on top. Fry at low heat for 30 seconds or so then flip the bread and repeat. The salt prevents burning and does not stick to the bread or pan. This is how our forefathers made toast on their wood-burning stoves.

To make campfire toast, scrape some coals away from the flames, level them out, and set your bread on top. Two seconds per side will do it!

WILD RICE PANCAKES

At the outset, I should say that with the exception of crepes and traditional blueberry hotcakes, I am not especially fond of pancakes, especially those which are made from a mix. But wild rice pancakes, which have been served for decades in the best backwoods camps, are the delicious exception.

Procedure: boil the wild rice in lightly salted water until it is done (about 45 minutes). Then, add a quarter pound of butter or margarine to each quart of cooked rice. Spoon a generous amount of cooked rice into your pancake batter and prepare the pancakes as you normally would. Top with hot maple syrup, cut 50 percent with butter or margarine. A sprinkle of cinnamon adds additional flavor.

Cooked wild rice that is kept refrigerated will keep for many days. Or, freeze left over rice and save it for use in pancakes on that special occasion.

SOURDOUGH PANCAKES AND BREADS

Sourdough pancakes are deliciously traditional, and are easy to make. Culturing the batter is easy. You can buy special "starters" or make your own. I prefer this easy do-it-yourself recipe.

Put about two cups of flour, one tablespoon sugar, and a teaspoon of vinegar into a stoneware crock or plastic bucket. Add enough warm water to make a thin, honey-like batter. Let the mixture work at room temperature for a week or more until it "sours", after which, it will be ready for use. As the dough sours, a clear yellowish liquid will float to the top of the mix. Occasionally, pour off the excess and replenish the mix with more flour and water. The souring dough will bubble and thicken, and begin to smell sour. Now, you're ready to make your pancakes.

Remove enough well-stirred liquid to make your pancakes and place it in a mixing bowl. Immediately replace the batter you took with fresh flour and water to prevent the mixture from over-souring. Add a pinch (no more!) of baking soda to the mix. Stir thoroughly and watch the batter rise and form a merIngue-like consistency.

Now, add a dash of salt, sugar to taste, one or two eggs, if you have them, and about three tablespoons of liquid shortening to the mix. Thin or thicken the batter, as necessary, by adding unsifted flour, water or milk. Fry the pancakes on medium heat and use as little oil (the shortening is in the mix) as possible.

Tips

1. If you prefer a milder, less sour tasting pancake, substitute dry flour and water for some of the sour-

dough. Too much baking soda spoils the taste; too little produces a flat cake. Leave out the soda if you prefer a dead flat, crepe-like pancake.

The procedure for making bread, biscuits or the traditional bannock, is similar to that outlined above except you must add flour to thicken the mix to bread dough consistency. Fold the flour gently into the biscuits, taking care not to overwork the dough. Do not knead sourdough. Doing so will make the bread tough and heavy.

2.   Add some flour and water to your crock pot every day or two. The mix will become useless and rancid—and may even explode!—if you don't you keep "feeding" it.

Some years ago, as a Forest Service employee, I maintained a sourdough bucket in a five gallon ice-cream can while stationed at a remote backwoods cabin in Oregon. One day, our crew was recruited to fight a forest fire many miles away. The clock was ticking: we had only minutes to grab essentials and catch the awaiting helicopter. Unbeknownst to me, a friend snapped down the cover on the sourdough bucket and set an iron skillet on top. When we returned to the cabin a week later, the bucket had exploded and there was sourdough all over the walls and ceiling. It took the better part of a day to clean up the mess.

Moral? Feed the beast every day, or refrigerate it!

3.   You can make the initial starter by substituting a cake of fresh yeast for the vinegar, if you prefer. But this isn't necessary. In fact, a mix of flour, water and sugar will often sour on its own without your help. If all this sounds too uncertain, a time-tested commercial starter may be right for you.

In 1991, 20 year old Scott Power and 19 year old David Scott over-wintered alone in a remote log cabin 100 air miles from Churchill, Manitoba. Smoking moose meat, falling through thin ice, suffering severe frostbite, being lost for a week at 40 below and experimenting with sourdough were part of the learning curve for the youthful explorers.

Less determined souls might have perished in the intense cold or buckled under the stress of spending a long arctic winter in a tiny lamp-lit cabin. But David and Scott followed their dream and returned to their Indiana home bronzed, fit, and wise beyond their years. Scott is currently writing a book about sourdough cooking, which is a passion. It will be published by ICS Books. Here, Scott urges backpackers to experience the delights of sourdough.

"Decades ago, sourdough was an equivalent to the American Express card—you didn't leave home without it. Within a crock of zesty, bubbling sourdough batter was the potential for mouth watering breads, biscuits, and of course pancakes—all while on the trail.

Nowadays though, in an age of quick to fix, dehydrated silver bag entrees like Turkey Tetrazzini, Beef Bourguignon and Cantonese Shrimp, who wants to deal with something that bubbles like an ooze, smells like beer but isn't, and could blow up in your pack at any given time unless properly stored? Who could possibly be crazy enough to pack such a thing as sourdough?

Me. I did and do, have and will, pack sourdough while in the bush.

Why mess with such a mess? Why inconvenience, complicate and confuse a backcountry belly? Because sourdough, if used well, can make a backwoods breakfast more fulfilling, a "middle-of-the-river" snack more tasty and even intensify the already "Nirvana" phenomenon people of the bush frequently experience.

Yea, it's possible that if not properly packed, the sourdough crock could either spill or explode in your pack, coating all your gear with sourdough starter. Yea, it takes practice to really make sourdough products well. Yea, sourdough will add extra weight to your already overloaded pack. But trust me, if you insist on taking something like a steel ammo can to pack out feces, or are concerned about enhancing your adventure with outdoor gear colored in teal, magenta or hot coral, sourdough is something you must give a chance. Your backcountry belly will thank you."

Scott Power

MAKING THE TRADITIONAL BANNOCK

French pastry not withstanding, the deliciously sweet, nutty, full-bodied aroma of a sourdough bannock, laced with fresh raisins and cinnamon, hissing and cackling before a hickory fire, is enough to rouse to breakfast the sleepiest of campers on the most miserable mornings.

Bannocks are fast and easy to make, and unlike other "woods breads", are not at all messy to prepare. Here's how to make a fresh-baked bannock that will put your cracker-carrying cronies to shame.

Sourdough bannock: follow the sourdough recipe above, adding enough flour to make a medium texture dough that will spread easily in a well-greased frying pan. With a spoon, spread the dough right to the edges of the skillet, then set the pan in the warm ashes of your fire for about 10 minutes to let the dough rise. Then, set the skillet directly over low flames or coals and slowly fry the bottom of the bannock, shuffling the pan from time to time to prevent burning.

When the bottom of the bannock is golden-brown, it's time to perform the theatrical part of the ceremony. Build the fire high and prop the fry pan about 45 degrees to the leaping flames. Occasionally rotate the skillet (or bannock) until the surface turns a uniform golden brown. Test for doneness with a sliver of wood shaved with your pocket knife.

There are hundreds of recipes for bannock, but by definition, all are made in a straight-sided, open frying pan. Sourdough makes the best tasting bannock, but Bisquick™ or other prepared baking-powder mixes are adequate.

The traditional bannock maker carries his or her prepared powder mix in a canvas or cotton bag into which a plastic bag has been first inserted. Old timers used to iron paraffin into unlined cloth bags to waterproof and stiffen them.

With a spoon, make a small depression in the center of the flour-mixture in the bag, and pour water directly into this depression. Mix the water, a little at a time, until the dough takes on a fairly stiff consistency but remains sticky to the touch. If you're careful, there'll be no flour clinging to the sides of the bag. Of course, you can perform this operation in a mixing bowl, but it won't impress your friends.

If you don't want to use sourdough or a commercial mix and prefer to start from scratch, place these ingredients into your "bannock bag":

Two cups of flour

Three rounded teaspoons of baking powder

One heaping tablespoon of non-fat dry milk (I prefer Milkman™ or Sanalac™).

One teaspoon of salt

Combine these ingredients with five tablespoons of liquid or melted shortening and mix thoroughly. Then, blend in two-thirds cup of cold water, carefully working the dough as little as possible to prevent toughness of the baked product. Place the well-mixed dough in your greased frying pan and proceed as before. It's not necessary to let the dough rise by the fire as with a sourdough bannock.

The secret to making good bannock is four-fold: 1) Don't make the batter too thick—one-half inch is enough. 2) Use a frying pan with rather straight sides so the bannock won't slide out when it's propped before the fire. 3) Don't use thin aluminum skillets which get too hot too quick. 4) Don't prop up the frying pan until the bottom of the bannock is well-browned.

Topped with honey and butter, bannocks are delicious with any meal. They add warmth and a touch of class to any meal.

TWIST ON A STICK

Every boy scout knows about "twist on a stick". Simply mix up a sticky, heavy-bodied batter and roll it between your hands to produce a long, snake-like mass. Then, twist the dough around a stick and bake it over the fire much as you would a hot dog. Sounds barbarian, but the result is as tasty as that produced by the most sophisticated convection ovens.

TORTILLA LEFSA

I hail from Minnesota where lefsa is an honored tradition. Serious Norwegian cooks still make the batter from scratch, while lazy folk like me just buy the pre-fab shells at the grocery store and micro-wave them. Topped with generous amounts of butter and brown sugar, the oven hot potato pastries are a taste sensation you'll never forget.

But how to make lefsa in the field? Store bought shells lack preservatives and spoil quickly, so preservative packed soft flour tortillas are the logical substitute. I lightly fry tortillas in margarine then immediately roll the sugar/margarine mixture inside. Blueberry or raspberry preserves adds additional flavor and calories. Tortillas also make a great stuffer for lunch meats and cheese. Lightly fried or baked with a variety of stuffings, they make tasty burritos.

COWBOY CAMP COFFEE

When water is at a rolling boil remove the kettle from the fire and add one tablespoon of fresh, fine ground coffee to the pot for each cup of coffee you plan to make. Stir the coffee into the hot water, cover and let steep for three minutes, then serve immediately. Set the pot near the fire or wrap it with clothes to keep it warm. Never boil or reheat coffee. Doing so will kill and bury a fine brew.

Coffee connoisseurs will note that this method of making camp coffee is nearly identical to the "cafetiere" and "pot" methods which are said to produce the best tasting coffee.

Tip: *for an interesting taste change, add a dash of cinnamon, almond, vanilla, or orange extract to your morning coffee.*

TRIPOD FISH

Old time camping books tout this method of preparing fish, though until I watched my good friend Dr. Bill Forgey do it at a remote campsite along Saskatchewan's Fond du Lac River, I would never have believed it worked.

Procedure: run a cord through the mouth/gills of a gutted (but not scaled or skinned) fish and hang the fish from a lashed together tripod. Build a roaring fire beneath the fish. The skin will blacken in the flames but the inner flesh will cook up chalky white. The meat is done when it flakes easily (about 15 minutes). Now, remove the tripod and fish, generously squirt the meat with lime or lemon juice, salt to taste, and go at it. Mmmm good! No pots, no mess, no fuss.

FRIED FISH

Pat dry fillets on paper toweling then roll them in flour or Bisquick™ that has been lightly seasoned with salt, pepper, garlic powder and paprika. Fry in sizzling hot peanut oil about six minutes or until golden brown. If you want thicker, crispier batter, roll the battered fillet in beaten egg then follow with a second coating of flour. For a sensational taste treat, salt lightly with "Cajun spice" and saute some diced onion in the pan before you fry each fillet.

Tip: *the blade of a canoe paddle or oar provides a flat surface for filleting fish.*

BOILED FISH

Scenario: The three pound walleye you caught is not enough to feed your crew. Should you fry it for yourself (selfish!) or throw it back (wasteful!)? Why, boil it up for supper, of course! *Procedure:* slice the fish fillets into bite-sized chunks. Drop the fish chunks into boiling soup or chowder and simmer for five minutes, no longer. Over-cooking will produce syrupy "lutefisk"; under-cooking may not kill all the harmful parasites. Boiled fish sounds awful but tastes wonderful. It is a regular staple on all my canoe trips above the tree line where I must conserve liquid fuel for my stove.

PLANKED FISH

Here's an easy way to prepare fish without utensils. Split a foot long chunk of log and hew one side relatively flat. Clean the fish, cut off the head, and split the body along the back. Then, peg the split fillets to the half-round log and set it before a roaring fire. Ten minutes of high heat will do the trick.

You can also cut the fish through the back and belly and suspend it—like an open book—from a simple rack above the fire. Keep the flame low so the fillets don't burn. Note: if possible, use hardwoods when baking fish or meat over an open fire. Resinous softwoods, like pine, spruce and fir, may impart objectional flavors into the food.

PEMMICAN AND RUBBABOO

The old Northwest fur Company did a lot of research on foods during the fur trade days of the 17th and 18th centuries and found that pemmican was the only food which a man could tolerate for long periods of time. The 18th century recipe usually consisted of pressed buffalo meat with a generous amount of buffalo grease added. Spencer Johnson, a teaching colleague, who belongs to an historic mountain man brigade, relies entirely on pemmican while deer hunting in the Minnesota woods. His formula provides as many calories and cholesterol as the original, but it contains readily available ingredients. Modern "high energy" bars may taste better, but few work as well as old time pemmican. Here is Spencer's modern recipe:

Mix equal parts of beef tallow (commercially processed suet), dried beef or venison, and dried fruit, like raisins or chopped up fruit roll-ups. Spence uses homemade deer jerky but chipped, dried beef works as well. Melt the fat and thoroughly mix it with the beef or venison and fruit. That's all there is to it. If the tallow is properly rendered, the pemmican should keep indefinitely. However, Spencer suggests that you err on the careful side by freezing what you don't use immediately.

The early voyageurs often mixed pemmican with flour, water, and sugar and cooked up a substantial soup called "rubbaboo", which they heartily devoured daily for weeks at a time. This traditional rubbaboo will feed four hungry campers:

> 2 pounds pemmican
>
> 2 cups of flour
>
> 4-5 cups of water
>
> 3/4 cup of sugar

Bring the pemmican and water to a boil, then blend in the flour and sugar. Simmer and stir constantly until the mixture is thick and smooth. You can improve the taste by substituting chipped dried beef and bacon fat for the pemmican, and by adding fruit, nuts and honey to the mix. The nature of the beast lends itself to considerable experimentation.

DEHYDRATING TRAIL FOODS

Lacking refrigeration, our eighteenth century forefathers naturally relied on a variety of dried meats and vegetables for their survival. Today, dehydrated and freeze-dried foods are as popular as fresh. Indeed, even fancy restaurants use some rehydrated products in their most expensive meals.

Whether or not it's worth slaving over a hot dehydrator to produce staples you can buy at any supermarket, depends on your perspective. Admittedly, you can probably purchase dried apples, bananas and fruit roll-ups at your local co-op for about the same cost as making them at home. Nonetheless, there's pride in self-sufficiency, which is reason enough to own a dehydrator.

I own an expensive dehydrator and for awhile dried everything. Now, I concentrate solely on hamburger, beef jerky, and fruit leather.

Hamburger provides the basis for a number of trail meals. With dried hamburger you can prepare spaghetti, chili, stroganoff, tacos, burritos, meat soups and stews. Freeze-dried hamburger costs more than a dollar an ounce and tastes no better in sauces than dry-it-yourself dehydrated stuff. The procedure is simple:

Brown raw hamburger and pour off the grease. Then, place the cooked hamburger in a strainer and pour boiling water over it to remove as much fat as possible. Line the dehydrator tray with 3-4 sheets of paper toweling and spread about one pound of well-drained hamburger on each tray. Turn the dehydrator to high (140° Fahrenheit) and let it run for 12 hours. That's all there is to it. For best results, package the hamburger immediately after drying. I use a vacuum sealing machine, but Ziplock bags work fine if you extract as much air as possible with a straw. Shelf life of vacuum sealed hamburger is about a year, four weeks for that stored in Ziplocks.

BEEF JERKY

There are many formulas for beef jerky. Here's one I can recommend:

1. You'll need about five pounds of high grade, lean steak for every pound of beef jerky you make. I've had good luck with round steak and venison.
2. Cut away every bit of fat, muscle and skin. Then cut the meat across the grain (following the meat's striation) in one-eighth inch thick strips.

Tip: *if you lightly freeze the meat it will slice more easily.*

3. Marinate the meat or rub in your favorite seasonings.

You can buy commercial seasonings or make your own. I've had excellent success with this marinade from Una Jean Peterson's book, *"Dehydrating for Food and Fun"*:

3 lbs beef strips

1 tsp. onion powder

1 tsp. garlic powder

1/2 tsp. pepper

1/3 c. Worcestershire sauce

1/4 soy sauce

1/2 tsp. hickory smoked salt.

Blend seasonings and pour over meat strips. Cover tightly and refrigerate for two hours. Stir or turn pieces frequently while marinating. Drain strips and load the trays to dehydrate.

Ms. Peterson suggests these precautions which I pass on to you:

1. Use aseptically clean cutting boards. Three-fourths cup of bleach mixed with a gallon of water is a good germicide.
2. Wash your hands and knife thoroughly before and after handling meats.

SMOKING MEAT AND FISH

Paddle a river in northern Canada or Alaska and at some point you're sure to see huge racks of luscious trout or salmon fillets drying in the afternoon sun. Sun-dried fish has for centuries been the staple of families who live in the bush.

Drying fish is so simple it almost needs no explanation. Clean the fish and cut off the heads. Then slice them up the back, stopping short of the tail so that a "hinge" of flesh remains. Now, suspend the split bodies from a rack and let the sun and wind do the work. On damp, windless days, you may need a light smoky fire to deter flies and help dry the meat. But keep your fire small: smoke, not heat is what you want! When rain comes, rig a crude roof and keep up the smoke. If it's hot and windy, the fillets may be dry and ready to eat in a day or two. Fish preserved in this manner will last for months.

The same procedure is used to dry fresh meat. Cut the strips thin—a quarter inch or less—and if necessary, use light smoke to keep the flies away. After about three hours, a tough coating which flies cannot penetrate, will form on the meat, and you can stop the smoke. The meat will be crumbly-dry in two or three days if conditions are right.

FRUIT LEATHER

Blend your favorite fruit or berries into a pulpy mass, add a sweetener and pour onto the dehydrator tray. The result is a taste treat everyone will enjoy. The hardest thing about making fruit leather is saving enough of the finished product for the trail. Most likely, you'll eat everything to the last scraping as it comes from the dehydrator tray.

All you need to make fruit leather is a blender, some plastic wrap, a flexible spatula, Scotch tape and a dehydrator.

Procedure: line the dehydrator tray with plastic wrap and tape the wrap firmly to the tray. Trim, or fold under, the edges of the wrap so they won't curl over the pureed fruit and slow the drying process.

Next, puree the fruit in your blender and add honey (preferred) or corn syrup to taste. You can substitute sugar for honey, if you wish, but the latter adds taste and flexibility to the leather. Peterson suggests that you add 25 percent applesauce to berry leathers to make them more supple. But you'll like the finished product even if you don't follow this advice.

Set the dehydrator to 125° Fahrenheit (medium heat), and check back in 8-12 hours. When the surface of the leather is dry, some people peel the leather off the plastic and turn it over to dry the back side. But I never bother. The leather is done when it is "sticky dry" to the touch.

Tip: *fruit leather is a great way to use up that leftover jam from your last canoe trip!*

Spaghetti sauce and tomato paste are easily made into leathers using the above procedure. The final touch is to roll up and freeze these vegetable leathers, then break or blend them into compact chips which can be easily poured from a poly bottle. Think about all the wonderful meals you can prepare with dehydrated hamburger and red and white sauce!

HOBIES

When I was a boy scout in the 1950's, hobies were the favorite "first night" meal of my patrol. Forty years later, I still make them at home because they are delicious, easy-to-prepare, and require no thought or cooking utensils. This traditional trail recipe will feed one ravenous teenager:

Ingredients: 1/2 pound hamburger, 1/2 onion, 1/3 medium green pepper, 1 stalk celery, 1/2 medium potato, 1 small tomato, salt and pepper to taste. For a gourmet touch, include fresh mushrooms, broccoli and water chestnuts. The ingredients are flexible, so feel free to experiment.

Procedure: slice the veggies and roll everything together in aluminum foil (shiny side in to better reflect heat). Carefully seal the edges so precious gravy won't drip through.

Set the hobie in the warm coals (no flames) of your fire, or bake it slowly in a dutch oven for 45 minutes to an hour. You won't believe how good this is!

COOKING AT HIGH ALTITUDE

Air pressure, as every high school science student knows, decreases as altitude increases, which means that the higher you go, the more time it will take to cook your food. For example, water which boils at 212° Fahrenheit (100°C) at sea level will—depending on local air pressure—boil around 201° Fahrenheit (94°C) a mile up. Doesn't sound like much cause for concern, and below 5,000 feet or so, it isn't. Beyond that, the rule is to increase cooking times about ten percent for every 1,000 feet of climb, or simply keep the heat on till the meal is done. The alternative is to use a pressure cooker, which reduces conditions to sea level or below. Lacking this, a tight-fitting lid will contain some steam and substantially speed cooking.

Tips: *If you pre-soak dried foods in cold water and slice fresh meats and vegetables as thin as possible, they'll cook much faster. As you gain altitude, you'll also want to decrease by a pinch, the amount of sugar and baking powder you use. But no matter, backwoods cooking is enough of an inexact science to preclude taking these matters too seriously. Do remember, however, to add more liquid at the start of cooking or replace that which boils out.*

COOKING WITH OCEAN WATER

In 1987, I led a canoe trip down the remote Burnside River, in the Arctic region of Canada. When we arrived at the estuary, it was nine pm. We had planned to paddle some 30 miles down the inlet to the mouth of the Hood River, where we would disembark and hike to Wilberforce Falls which, at a height of 160 feet, is the highest falls north of the Arctic Circle. But it was too far to paddle non-stop, so we decided to camp and continue on the next day.

Two hours later, we found a decent campsite on a relatively solid mud flat. It was while preparing supper that I realized that the distinctly brackish ocean water was marginally potable, and we had only about a gallon of fresh water between the six of us. The decision was clear: we'd stretch our fresh water supply by boiling the spaghetti noodles in sea water.

For the next two days, we relied on varying proportions of sea water for cooking our meals. We discovered that a diluted (to taste) mix of fresh and salt water worked fine for making soups, stews and pasta. A scant pinch of sugar tamed the slight bitterness we experienced when making the pasta dishes.

Admittedly, our trip confined us to the brackish estuary of Bathurst Inlet. Farther out on the Arctic Ocean we would have experienced much saltier water. But the lesson was clear: cooking with sea water was a safe and practical way to extend the limits of our fresh water supply.

FOOD PREPARATION TIPS

The concentrated heat from a trail stove is apt to burn cereals and soups, no matter how much you stir. One solution is to use a "flame dissipator" of some sort. A tin can lid or tightly woven stainless steel screen placed on the burner head will effectively do the trick. Another option is the "three minute boil". Procedure: stir constantly as you bring the mush to a rolling boil. Keep stirring as you turn down the heat to the lowest possible blue-flame setting, and simmer for three minutes. Then, remove the pot from the stove and wrap warm clothes around it to conserve heat, as suggested in the last chapter.

Finally, I advise you not to take recipes too seriously. If you don't have items needed to make a meal, either leave them out or substitute generic equivalents. No sugar? Use honey, maple syrup, or sweetened powdered drink mix instead. Out of pancake syrup? Try melted peanut butter or warm jam. Not enough flour for bread? Mix in leftover breakfast mush; add re-hydrated fruit, brown sugar, jam, cinnamon and nuts, and you'll have a tasty fruit and nut bread that everyone will enjoy.

Tips

1.   Your salt shaker won't clog up in damp weather if you add about 20 percent rice to it.

2.   Fresh green peppers, tomatoes, and other vegetables will last much longer in the backcountry if you soak them in a dilute solution of bleach and water for 15 minutes before you pack them away. I use 10 drops of chlorine bleach to a quart of water, which is more than twice the recommended dosage for purifying cold or cloudy water. I always rinse treated veggies in clear water before I prepare them, even though health authorities tell me this isn't necessary. As mentioned in the last chapter, fresh, dry vegetables are best carried in cotton or paper bags, and packed so they won't bruise. Never

seal fresh vegetables in plastic or metal foil: the humid environment that results will promote fast spoilage.

3.   Don't take the directions too seriously when preparing freeze-dried and dehydrated foods. Doing so may result in over-cooked meat and pulpy vegetables. Instead, pre-soak hard-to-cook ingredients in cold water for up to 20 minutes before you cook them. Then, use the "time-layered" (Wok) system to prepare them; i.e., cook hard items first, soft items last.

For example, I start dried meat in cold water then simmer for several minutes before adding veggies which, when cooked, signify that the meal is done.

Tip: *to soften sinewy meat, pound flour into it.*

And finally, here's a tip for running an efficient outdoor kitchen: The first thing you should do when you set up camp is to establish the location of the kitchen and assemble all food and cooking gear in that area. Except for one or two "cook's helpers", everyone who is not involved in food-making should stay away. Well-meaning friends are naturally curious, but their presence (and chatter!) disrupts organization of the meal—not to mention the dirt that will fall into pots as they stroll by. Besides, there's a certain mystique that goes along with preparing fine food, and no good cook wants to give away his or her trade secrets!

CHAPTER

four

• • •

A Cut Above the Rest

Everything You Need to Know About Choosing Edged Tools

THE CONTROVERSIAL HATCHET

An admirer once asked Daniel Boone's friend, Simon Kenton, to name three items he'd most want to have along on a lengthy trek across the "dark and bloody ground". "Rifle and tommyhawk," replied Simon wistfully . . . "Then maybe m'Green River knife or fire-steel. I'd have to think on it."

Hand-axe, short-axe, hatchet, or tomahawk. Whatever you call it, variations on the theme have been around in one form or other for at least 200,000 years. No other cutting tool has proven as versatile, or as controversial.

To most outdoors people, a hand-axe is a dangerous toy—inferior to a full size axe for bringing down big timber or splitting wood, and too short to deflect a glancing blow while chopping. Cut fingers, feet and shins, are par for the course wherever hatchets are found which, sadly enough, is usually in the hands of well-meaning youngsters. Even when all safety precautions are followed, hand-axes can slip. And cut! Reason enough to ban them from every summer camp in the land, and the pages of nearly all outdoors books.

Denunciations are poignant: "Now a hatchet is a dangerous thing . . . the term 'hatchet job' . . . refers to the poor quality of work and frequent self-mutilation that usually occurs when the instrument is used for chopping wood" (from *The Joy of Camping,* by Richard Langer). Or, "Hatchets and other miniatures are poor substitutes (for a big axe), indeed worse than no substitute at all. Not only are they not up to the job of bringing down big wood, they force the user to flail at his target with brute strength" (*The Complete Wilderness Paddler,* James West Davidson and John Rugge).

Given this glowing testimony, how is it that the lowly hand-axe has been able to survive a quarter million years of uninterrupted production? Only the fixed blade hunting knife and skin drum can share that honor. Could our ancestors have developed a skill with this tool that we've long forgotten? Or, do we expect the hand-axe to perform tasks for which it was never intended? Perhaps a short lesson in American history will uncover the truth.

"Tomahawk" is an Algonquian word for a club or throwing type of weapon. The original tomahawks consisted of a carved wooden club about two feet long, into which was set a ball of stone, wood or bone. Whatever the substance, its function was clear: it was designed to kill people! Certainly, tomahawks were, on occasion, used in the hunt, but that was never their primary intent.

Fleshing hides and downing trees required more efficient tools than stone tomahawks. Large trees were slowly burned down. Primitive man packed clay around the trunk to prevent the flames from spreading. Then, he built a hot fire beneath and infrequently nursed along the project with artful swipes of his dull stone tomahawk.

When, in the 16th century, Europeans introduced the steel tomahawk, battle efficiency, but not general use of the weapon, changed significantly. Steel tomahawks were lighter and faster to swing than their stone predecessors and so added a measure of finesse to the unruly game of battle. But the labor of felling large trees was still the domain of the fire and clay ring. Tomahawks were simply too small and light for the drudgery of clearing land.

Then came a revolution. Some time in the 1600's, a clever European offered to the Indians trade axes with more "useful" heads—heads, which in fact, closely resembled the modern Hudson bay style axe. The "trade tomahawk" was ground thin for efficient chopping, and some expensive models even sported built-in peace pipes.

"Pipe axes" were highly regarded by Indian braves, while more utilitarian models were cherished by Indian women for such unmanly pursuits as splitting kindling and pounding teepee pegs. Voilá! The modern hatchet was born. From here, it was but a short jaunt to polished steel heads and vinyl-wrapped handles.

From splitting skulls and pounding heads, to cutting kindling and hammering pegs—all in just 300 years. Noble evolution? Perhaps. But never once along the way was the weapon ever viewed as a serious chopping tool.

Bringing down big wood is the domain of the saw, as is ripping it into stove lengths. Full size axes—alá those with 28–32 inch handles—are useful for hacking dead stumps, splitting fireplace wood, and blazing wilderness trails. The big axe continues to play an important role in backwoods camping, as we'll see shortly. But it is the modern short-axe (hatchet) which is most useful to on-the-move campers.

To summarize, the primary function of modern hatchets is to produce kindling for small campfires. Some tent stake pounding still goes on, though skewer type aluminum stakes have eliminated most of that. To its list of uses we might also add setting rivets in torn pack straps, attaching snaps to field clothing and camping gear, straightening bent aluminum hardware on damaged canoes and fishing boats, field dressing (hacking the bones of) large animals killed in the hunt, and scraping hides.

As you can see, the modern hatchet ably performs a diversity of outdoor tasks. But its greatest value is in making a camp fire after a week long rain. Since all wood that's small enough to be broken by hand is apt to be thoroughly soaked, the solution is to cut a dead, downed log into foot long sections with a folding saw, then to split this wood (to get at the dry center) with a hand-axe. Simply set the log chunk on end and lightly bury the hatchet blade into the end grain. Hold the handle tightly with both hands while a friend pounds the head on through with a chunk of log (hammer). What could be easier? Or safer?

STORING, CARRYING AND SHEATHING YOUR AXE

Scenario: a well-ordered campsite at dusk. Near the tightly pitched tent is a bright, smoke-free fire, around which good friends are chatting and drinking coffee. In the foreground, a hand axe is safely (??) buried into a dead downed log.

Lazily, a man crawls out of the tent and clumsily trips over the dark-colored guy line. He falls onto the axe and dislodges the blade which causes a freak "axident". Suddenly, what was a nonchalant vacation is now a medical emergency!

Though traditional camping texts tout the "bury-it-in-the-log" method as safe, experienced axe users know better. The two safe places to store an axe are 1) in its sheath, 2) blade under a log as illustrated in figure 4-1.

Sheathing the Axe   Factory sheaths are an abomination. Make a sturdy sheath from heavy sole leather or slit a piece of garden hose and secure it to the blade with a band cut from an innertube. Your shoe repair man can sell you the materials you need or make a sheath for you in a few minutes. Safety concerns suggest that an axe sheath is better riveted than sewn.

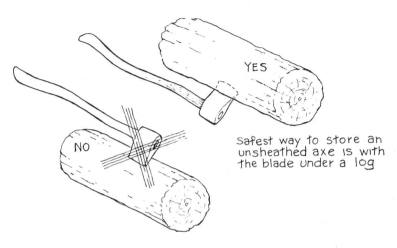

Safest way to store an unsheathed axe is with the blade under a log

Figure 4-1

CAMP SAWS

Except for splitting wood and certain log cabin building chores, there's nothing an axe can do that a sharp camp saw can't do better. But get a saw hung up in a log, and you'll wish you had an axe to chop it free.

Regrettably, the practical wood-frame bucksaw of the last century has gone the way of the passenger pigeon. More than a thing of beauty, it could be adjusted for tension, and completely dismantled for carrying. In its place is the fixed-blade all-steel bow saw which cannot be disassembled or adjusted. Nonetheless, the bow saw works well enough. It is strong and inexpensive—the logical choice for a semi-permanent camp where portability or longevity is not a concern.

Best portable camp saw I've found is the Fast Buck-Saw™, which is a compact, modern version of the old wood frame bucksaw. The one pound tool is constructed of hard maple and has an easily replaceable 21 inch hardware store blade. Recently top rated by *Country Journal* Magazine, this furniture grade saw is available from Fast BuckSaw, Inc. 110 E. Fifth St., Hastings, MN 55033.

A new, all aluminum folding saw which I can heartily recommend, is the Sawvivor™. Available from Dawn Marketing, Inc., 474 Genesee St., Avon, NY 14414 (phone: 1–800–724–3529), the 10.5 ounce "bucksaw" assembles in seconds and has room to store two 15″ blades inside the frame. A captive tensioning system ensures tight, positive lockup. Developed by two avid backpackers who are also engineers, Sawvivor™ is the easiest to use and most efficient full frame compact saw I've seen.

There are also a number of short-bladed pruning saws which open and close like jack-knives. These little saws are fine for cutting small branches but are too flimsy for woodpile work.

At the bottom of the useful list are wire "survival" saws and toothed Swiss army knife blades which, in a pinch might save the day. Carry them if you wish, but not in place of a "real" saw.

SAW SAFETY AND MAINTENANCE

1. Support the saw log at one end only, as illustrated in figure 4-2a. Even a relatively light log will cause the saw blade to bind if you support the log at both ends.

2. Undercut long, "stress-bent" logs. If you must cut stress-bent logs from the top, use a light aluminum wedge to keep the cut from binding.

3. The bright, carbon steel blade of a camp saw will rust in short order if you don't keep it well-oiled. WD-40 is an excellent rust-inhibitor and honing oil.

4. Tree sap will inhibit cutting performance. Remove sap with liquid fuel, alcohol, or WD-40.

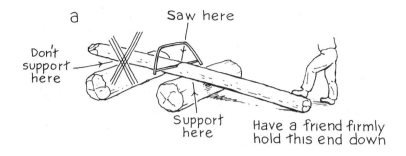

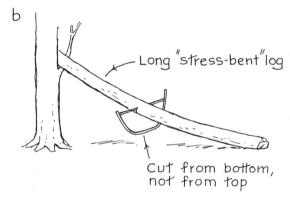

Figure 4-2

KNIVES

When I was a kid, every camper carried a long bladed "hunting" knife. Not wishing to follow the crowd, I saved for a year to buy a legendary Puma Plainsman—a premium lockback folder which is similar to the excellent Buck folding hunter.

Then, in the 1960's, there came a revolution. Suddenly, everyone discovered the Swiss army knife—everyone, that is, except wise scoutmasters and boy scouts who preferred the strength and awesome sharpness of the original tool steel Camilus "Boy Scout knife." Camilus still makes these tough old knives, which are excellent if you like a multipurpose folder.

Spend much time in the woods and you quickly learn what makes a good knife. Here, in no particular order, are my parameters:

1. A fixed blade of 4–5 inches provides enough length to slice cheese and meats, and to reach to the bottom of the peanut butter bottle without gumming up the hilt.

2. Flat ground blade. Flat sided knives are best for slicing meats and spreading jam and peanut butter.

3. Blade thickness across the spine must be no greater than one-eighth of an inch. Three-thirty-seconds is better. Finding a sheath knife with a blade that thin isn't easy: most fixed blade knives are chisel-thick and designed for skinning rhinos—exactly what you don't want for general camping.

4. The blade is best made from high carbon tool steel. Stainless steel is difficult and expensive to work and even more difficult to sharpen to a razor edge. If stainless was as good as some knife-makers proclaim, they'd make wrenches out of it! Fact is, properly tempered tool steel is by far the best material for a serious working knife. Granted, tool steel requires care, but so does a fine gun or fishing reel. Once you've used (and sharpened!) a quality tool steel knife, you'll never go back to stainless steel.

Stainless blades are popular because you can throw them in a tackle box and leave them for years, and they won't rust away. Fact is, the daily chore of oiling and sharpening a knife is a forgotten art. An Orvis fly rod is worth babying, and so is a razor sharp tool steel knife. Finding an honestly useful "camp knife" today isn't easy. Here are some excellent knives I can honestly recommend:

Gerber Shorty: possibly, the best camp knife ever offered by a commercial company, the Shorty features a 3/32" thick flat ground chrome-plated tool steel blade that's hardened to 60 on the Rockwell scale. The comfort contoured aluminum handle is fused on and covered with non-slip material. A homely, futuristic looking tool, the Gerber is practical at home and in the field. Low sales recently prompted discontinuation of this excellent knife, which can occasionally be found in some stores.

All of the Schrade "Old Timer" knives are constructed from tough, easy-to-sharpen tool steel. Schrade makes an inexpensive lock-back folding hunter (it has a pressure spring) that has a thin, flat-ground blade, which can be honed to shaving sharp in a matter of minutes. Case and Camilus also make some impressively built tool steel knives which are much better than the ones grand-dad used.

Tip: single-bladed knives offer the best value for the dollar. If you need a tool shop, buy a precision ground Leatherman™ tool. With it, you can tighten the mini-screw on your glass frames, cinch the Phillips on your fishing reel, extract—or cut—the hook from the mouth of a killer pike, file the edge of your axe, open a can, pierce leather and more. Unlike knife-style competitors, the Leatherman™ has tools you can heartily rely on when the chips are down. For me, a Leatherman and Gerber Shorty are the ideal belt tools.

Any of the Ruana™ thin-bladed "stickers". Rudy Ruana, America's second oldest custom knife-maker, passed away a few years ago. His son-in-law, Vic Hangas, carries on the tradition. Until a decade ago, Vic and Rudy re-tempered and hand-forged old Studebaker springs. Now, Hangas specifies the finest hi-carbon tool steel. Blades are free hand ground, individually oil quenched and heat treated. Handles are aluminum, cast on the tang, with elk horn inserts beveled and riveted. The thin-bladed four inch "sticker" is a fine camp knife, though it is hollow ground. Ruana knives are ridiculously underpriced. Demand for them is so high, there is no need to advertise. But you can get details by writing Ruana Knife Works, Box 520, Bonner, Montana 59823.

In the 1940's, Western Cutlery manufactured a practical work knife for the Navy's legendary Construction Battalion, the Sea-bee's. The original "Sea-bee" knife had a 5 inch long, tapered flat-ground, tool steel blade that measured just 3/32" across the spine. Handle material was stacked leather washers capped by an oversized polished steel pommel which could be used for pounding light nails.

An exact copy of the original blued-steel "Sea-bee" is now available from Western Cutlery. A heavy duty military sheath (stamped USN) comes with the knife. The thin carbon steel blade quickly takes a razor edge and slices cheese and sausage wafer thin. A summer of heavy use in the Canadian wilds convinced me that this classic old knife is one of the most practical camp knives around. Note: the practical, plain Jane looks of this 1940's working knife suggest it won't be popular with drugstore cowboys, so don't expect to find a Sea-bee at your local hardware store. However, any Coleman-Western dealer can order the knife for you.

Buck™ makes a small, thin-bladed little knife called the "Scout", which is ideal for most camp chores. Buck steel (which has been characterized as a "modified stainless") is strong and stain-resistant but it is very hard to sharpen.

Consumer Reports magazine recently gave Chicago Cutlery™ kitchen knives top honors. Some models with 4–5 inch blades make ideal camp knives, if you make a sheath for them.

MAKE A SHEATH FOR YOUR KNIFE

The military pattern sheaths which come with fixed blade knives are insecure and awkward to use. The "holster style" case developed by the Indians and Eskimos is safer and more practical. Here's how to make a classy, form-fitted holster for your knife:

1.   Obtain some heavy sole leather from Tandy Leather Company. Knife sheath kits are available, but the leather that's supplied with them is too thin for backwoods use.

2.   Soak the leather in water for a few minutes to soften it. While the leather is wet, mold and cut it to the shape of the tool (you should make a paper pattern, first).

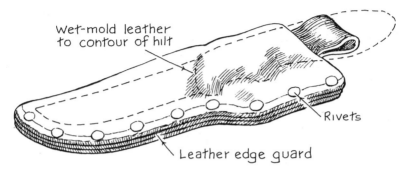

Wet-mold leather
to contour of hilt

Rivets

Leather edge guard

Figure 4-3

3. When the leather is dry enough to hold its shape, mold it around the blade and hilt. The leather should cover all but the top one-third of the handle.

4. Allow the leather to dry for an hour then glue (use waterproof contact cement) a quarter-inch wide strip of scrap leather along the edge. This "edge guard" will prevent the blade from cutting into stitching or rivets.

    Sew or rivet on a belt loop then rivet or sew up the sheath. A shoemaker can stitch the leather for you in a few minutes. If you prefer to do the job yourself, you'll need two leather needles and waxed thread (available from Tandy Co.). Mark each stitch hole then drill it through with a needle-thin bit. Or, forget this foolishness and simply hammer down two-piece, nickle-plated, brass rivets which are also available from the Tandy Company.

5. Wet down the finished sheath and insert the knife into it (the blade should be thickly covered with rust inhibiting grease). Use heavy finger pressure

to mold the leather to the contours of the knife. When the sheath has dried, the knife should slide in and out with an audible "click".

6.   Last step is to apply several coats of shoe polish. Never use "boot grease" (it softens leather) on knife or axe sheaths.

CHAPTER

five

• • •

Mending the Tears

How to Repair and Prolong the Life of Your Gear

The portage began in a marginally protected cove dangerously close to the lip of the ten meter falls. Whipped by mild eddy currents, the rocky shore provided only enough space for one canoe to land at a time. So as soon as my partner and I had put ashore, we dragged our 18 foot Grumman well up the bank to make room for our friends. As a precautionary measure, we tied the bow line to a tree, certain our friends would follow suit.

Two trips over the portage and everything was across. One man had turned an ankle on a previous carry, so I went back to fetch his canoe.

When I arrived at the start, the Alumacraft was gone. Perhaps Roger had brought it over by a different route. No matter, it was a nice day and I didn't mind the hike. As I ambled into the sunlit opening which marked the start of the carry, a friend sauntered up.

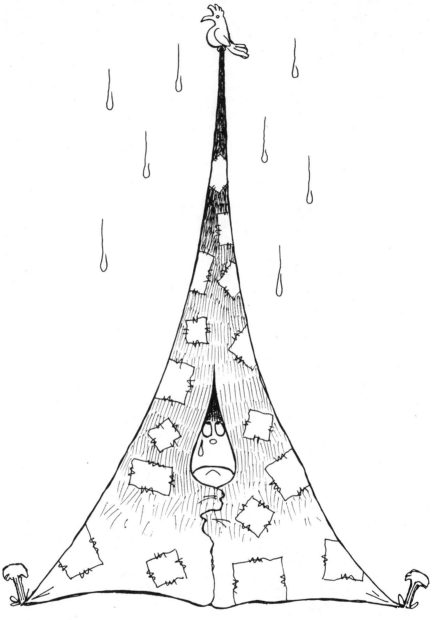

Figure 5-1

"Hey Cliff, ya seen the Alumacraft?"

"Nyah, someone must've gotten it."

"Ain't on the other side."

"You guys tie it up?" I asked.

A long pause and then . . . "Oh my God, I'll bet it went over the falls!"

A queasiness rose upward from the pit of our stomachs and surfaced as panic. Here we were, deep in the Ontario bush, 80 miles from the nearest road, and we'd just lost a boat. How on earth could we pile six men and three weeks of camping gear into two canoes? Numbed by the seriousness of the situation, we ran intently back over the trail, our eyes glued to the thundering cascade, vaguely hoping to see a glint of shiny white metal. There was none. Our worst fears were realized: the canoe had submarined in a deep current and was wedged into the rocks.

For awhile we just stood at the base of the drop and stared wishfully at the run-out below. Then, out of nowhere, a swamped, twisted canoe surfaced and floated mystically towards us. Dumbfounded by the sight, no one said anything until I hooked a gunnel of the battered craft with the T-grip of my paddle. Then, suddenly, the seriousness of concern gave way to frivolous hollers of delight. What might have been a tragedy was averted by a generous share of good luck.

Together, we surveyed the damage. The bow deck plate was half torn off and two rivets were pulled loose from the deeply bent keel. The gunnel line was no longer symmetrical and a front seat weld had broken. But the hull was sound as a dollar. Glory be, we could repair it!

First priority was to straighten the keel, which we did by jumping on the hull from the inside. A chunk of log and repeated blows from a handaxe acceptably reformed the gunnel curve. Fixing the pulled rivets was not so easy as the break had occured on the curve of the stem. Fortunately, I had a small steel drift punch in my tool kit. A few whaps with the backside of my axe and the rivet holes were clear, albeit, now oversized.

I had no matching aluminum rivets, so two piece brass rivets from Tandy leather company would have to do. These fit sloppily into the holes but were long enough to seal. A glob of ugly black shoe goop, plus a protective covering of duct tape provided a watertight seal.

Next, we hammered down the deck plate, filed off the rough edges and set two self-tapping metal screws into the distorted rivet holes.The final touch was to bolt down the seat. An hour later, the old Alumacraft was up and running. It negotiated the remaining 200 miles to James Bay without a hitch.

BUILDING A PERSONAL TOOL KIT

If you've done your homework before paddling a wild river, you'll never need to repair a damaged canoe. But what if a tent pole snaps or a zipper breaks? Suppose a pack strap tears or you hole your rubber boots? Got a bad leather washer in your liquid fuel stove? Can you make a new one from materials on hand, or will you have to take a cutting from your boot tongue? Do you have the tools to field-strip your fishing reel or tighten your eye glasses? Even broken canoe paddles and axe handles can be repaired in the back-country if you have the right stuff. Here's a run down of what you'll want along on your next backwoods adventure.

FOR CLOSE-TO-HOME MINI-ADVENTURES

For predictable outings, a Swiss army knife and duct tape are probably enough. Add a sturdy pliers with a cutting edge and a pounding tool (handaxe) of some sort, and you'll be well prepared for most emergencies.

For an ultra-compact kit, I recommend the versatile "Leatherman" tool, mentioned in chapter 4. With it, you can field strip eye glasses, fishing reels, or a fine shotgun. Its powerful pliers easily snip fishhooks and heavy wire. There's a small but useful file, an awl, can opener and cap lifter, a Phillips and three precision ground flat screwdrivers. So good is the "Leatherman", that on go-light trips in Minnesota, it is the only tool that many snow-mobilers carry. Outdoor Equipment Review magazine (no longer published), whose testing format was similar to that of "Consumer's Reports", said the "Leatherman" was the most useful multi-tool they had seen. And as an added bonus, the "Leatherman" is made in America.

TOOLS FOR SERIOUS TRIPS

These tools weigh under two pounds and will fit in a 9″×5″ zippered case:

One four inch long crescent wrench: You need the power and dexterity of a true wrench to tighten bolts on stoves, boats and machinery. The tiny crescent, with its 5/8 inch opening, handles most camp chores. Use it as a mini-clamp when gluing small items.

A long nose pliers with side-cutter and a 5-1/2 inch standard pliers. Or, you can substitute a Leatherman for these items. Two pliers, or a wrench and pliers, are often needed to free stubborn bolts, so don't skimp here.

Steel, coin-style gun screwdriver. These inexpensive half-dollar sized screwdrivers have three precision bits that will fit the tiny screws in fishing reels and eye glasses. Again, no need for this tool if you carry a "Leatherman".

A few steel bolts and nuts. Bolts seldom break, but matching nuts may work loose and be lost. Carry sizes to match the rivets and bolts in your equipment.

Some assorted wood screws and self-tapping metal screws: useful for mending broken wood, metal and fiberglass.

A small, adjustable C-clamp enables you to glue broken parts more accurately.

A half dozen assorted size rivets. The double-headed, hammer-set ones available from Tandy Leather Co., are ideal for repairing pack straps, and, in an emergency, aluminum canoes.

Silver duct tape or one of the better modern equivalents. Rewind a half inch or so on a wooden dowel and keep it in your repair kit. Duct tape should be available when you need it, so wind some more around a pack frame member or canoe thwart.

Though duct tape is the traditional repair item for everything that fails in the backcountry, a small roll of nylon filament tape is better for reinforcing cracks in paddles, oars and tool handles.

A half dozen heavy-duty glove snaps and setting tool will repair a broken raincoat zipper or canoe splash cover.

Spare leather washer and fuel cap for your liquid fuel stove.

Tube of "Super Glue" for mending eye glass frames and other small items.

Five-minute epoxy is useful for mending broken tool handles, canoe paddles and oars. I carry a piece of fiberglass cloth in case I need to cement a paddle shaft or yoke bar in my canoe. Fiberglass can also be used to cover holes in tool sheaths and leather boots.

Shoe goop: best stuff around for fixing holes in boot soles. Also seals rivets and bolts in boats.

A curved, fine pointed dental tool is handy for "nitpicking" chores like removing rubber gaskets and jets in trail stoves.

One eighth inch diameter "gimlet". A gimlet is nothing more than a hand operated twist drill. I purchased the tool from The Brookstone Company in a size to match the bolts on my wood-trimmed canoe. I figured that if I ever broke a rail, I could drill new holes with the gimlet and wood-pin and epoxy the woodwork back together.

It was a noble idea. However, when I did wrap my Kevlar canoe around a midstream boulder in Canada, some years ago, the rails held fast. I've carried the gimlet for ten years now and have never used it. But dreams are the stuff of which wilderness trips are made and a drill of some sort still sounds like a good idea.

Cotton, Cordura, canvas, and leather for repairing pack-sacks and clothing.

Needles and thread. Include two large-eye sailmaker needles and some heavy, waxed thread. Dental floss and monofilament fishing line work great for sewing leather and canvas.

Small steel drift punch for removing broken rivets, bolts and screws.

A foot of three-quarter inch wide "sticky-back" Velcro. If you blow a zipper out of your tent or clothing, the quick stick Velcro will provide a reliable closure that's easy to install.

A metal zipper slider that's matched to the zipper on your tent. If a bug zipper goes in black fly country, you'll need more than Velcro to fix it. More often than not, zipper failure is the result of an over-stressed slider which has loosened from overuse. So before you commit to replacing the entire slider (which requires cutting the zipper), try tightening it with a pair of pliers, as suggested below.

Apply gentle, even pressure to each wing of the slider. Don't press too hard! The tempered metal is brittle and may break or jam if you exercise an Atlas touch. Then, lubricate the tightened slider with silicone or WD-40 before you try it. In a pinch, use cooking oil or margarine. Be aware that every time you tighten a slider you weaken the metal. Most sliders will break after the second tightening cycle, and will have to be replaced in the field by the following procedure.

1. Lubricate the stuck slider and carefully work (you may need a pliers) it to within one-fourth inch of the sewn down end of the track. Then, cut the zipper above the slider, remove the slider and install a new one.

2. Sew both sides of the cut track tightly together above the new zipper slider. You'll lose a half inch of travel on your zipper but otherwise it will work fine.

Include some *medium grade sandpaper* in your kit. You'll be amazed at how handy it is. Uses include smoothing the surface of stubborn tent pole joints, removing rust from the handaxe blade, roughing the surface of a rubber boot to accept a patch, polishing out food-retaining scratches in aluminum cookware or a splintery surface on an oar or canoe paddle; removing a burr from the lip of a polyethylene bottle, or leveling shards of broken gel-coat on your boat. The list goes on.

A ten inch smooth mill file is something else you'll want to have along. Use it for sharpening the axe and for deburring the end of damaged tent poles, slotted screws, or pinched boot eyelets. The small file on a Leatherman is no match for this hardware store item. The file and handaxe are the only tools that won't fit in my tool kit.

Traditional camping texts place copper wire and chewing gum high on the list of essentials. But there's nothing these items will do that shoe goop, duct tape and steel bolts won't do better.

You can assemble a more sophisticated tool kit than is suggested here, but additional items are probably overkill. All of which suggests that a field repair kit should contain the minimum equipment you need to effect "reliable" emergency repairs, and nothing more. Later, at home, you can use bench mounted equipment and the services of experts to fix things right.

EQUIPMENT CARE AND REPAIR

Woolens, down, and polyester-filled products

Woolens: Advertising to the contrary, wool is still the premiere material for outdoor travel. Good wool clothing can be worn day in and day out for years and retain its insulative value and new look. And wool has a much wider temperature comfort range than any of the synthetics, which means you'll sweat less when you work hard or when the day warms up. Best of all, wool does not absorb odors readily. The perspiration it does accumulate is easily washed out (without soap) in cold water. An hour of sun-drying usually renders the garment odor-free.

Polyesters, polypropylene's and garments of mixed synthetic blood must be washed in cold water with full-blooded detergent to eliminate all odors. Nonetheless, synthetic clothing has wide appeal, especially for use in winter and where light weight and fast-drying are important concerns. The battle over which fabric—wool or synthetic—is best, rages on. You'll find additional arguments on the issue in chapter 6.

However, when it comes to cleaning wool, polyester, and polypropylene, there is complete agreement. Wool may be dry-cleaned or washed. Synthetics must be washed. Contrary to popular belief, special wool soaps aren't necessary. Any mild detergent works fine. The key is to use cold or lukewarm water and avoid rough handling. Shirts are spun-dry in the machine then hung on wooden hangers out of direct sunlight to dry. Sweaters are laid flat on absorbent towels. Virgin wool is resilient; it can be stretched or shrunk to shape.

For example, the sleeves on most shirts are too long for me, so I shrink the sleeves by soaking them in very hot water for three minutes. The shirt is then spun-dry and placed in a "hot" clothes dryer. Careful monitoring (every three minutes) of the drying process produces the exact sleeve length I want. The pre-shrunk sleeves hold their shape for the lifetime of the garment. This procedure is not unique: for years lobster fishermen have "boiled" their wool mittens to make them warmer and more resistant to wind. And the world-famous "Dachstein" mittens and sweaters are shrunk to shape by a similar process.

Down-filled products: Never dry-clean down garments. Doing so—especially with perchloroethylene—will remove the natural oils and reduce loft. Here's an easy way to wash your down sleeping bag or jacket.

Machine wash the garment in a commercial *front loading* washing machine. Top-loading machines may destroy the delicate baffles. Use cold water and mild soap or detergent. I've had good luck with Ivory Flakes, Woollite, Basic-H, and Ivory dish-washing liquid. Special clear-rinsing down soaps are useful but not essential.

Pre-sponge gritty spots with a strong solution of detergent and water. I have used pre-wash stain removers like "Shout" on the grungy head area of my $300 down sleeping bag with no ill effects. However, manufacturers suggest that you use these products sparingly, if at all. Never use cleaning solvents, like those designed for removing carpet stains. Harsh chemicals will destroy your down sleeping bag!

When the washing machine stops, run it through a second cycle, only this time eliminate the soap. Most of the problems associated with washing down gear are the result of incomplete rinsing.

If the laundromat has an "extractor" (high-speed centrifuge), use it to remove the final rinse water. One pass through the extractor will remove nearly all the water.

Dry the sleeping bag in a large commercial dryer. Small home driers concentrate the heat over too small an area and may damage your bag. Set the dryer on the lowest possible heat setting and add a couple of tennis balls or sneakers with the laces removed to break up the down clumps.

Caution: The rubber or plastic in some tennis balls or shoes may melt from the heat of the dryer and cause irreparable damage to your down garment. For this reason, I suggest you place these items inside a cotton bag or sock before you put them into the dryer. Check the dryer frequently to be sure it really puts out LOW heat. If you can't control the temperature, wedge a magazine in the door safety switch so the machine will run (and bleed heat) while the door is slightly ajar. Stop the dryer every ten minutes or so and check the bag. Complete drying takes about two hours.

I generally wash my sleeping bags every 2–3 years by this method. My favorite bag, which is over 20 years old, looks and feels like new. Good quality goose down is resilient: you'll wear out the nylon shell of your sleeping bag long before you wear out the down.

HOW TO WASH SYNTHETICS

Polyester and polypropylene should never be dry cleaned because the solvents can melt the fibers. Machine washing, as for down, is by far the best procedure. Dirty polypropylene smells bad, doesn't insulate well, and pills readily. Undergarments should be washed every few days on a wilderness trip. Outer garments can be machine washed when you get home. Note that woolens can remain dirty for weeks without significantly affecting their performance or longevity. You'll prolong the life of all your garments if you dry them in strong sunlight for several minutes each day of your trip. Ultraviolet light kills the molds and bacteria which produce odors.

Storage: in between outings, store down and polyester sleeping bags and garments in oversize, porous stuff sacks (a pillow sack works fine) or on padded hangers. Don't keep these items confined in watertight bags for long periods. Sustained compression of the filling can permanently reduce loft.

To patch garments and sleeping bags, sew on a patch of matching material, which is often more difficult than it sounds, because "matching material" isn't always easy to find. Many down and polyester products come with nylon stuff sacks made of identical fabric, and I'm not above cutting these up to get the patching material I need. Most stuff sacks that come with sleeping bags and jackets are too small, anyway. Making a new oversized stuff sack is pleasant "winter work".

There are some excellent modern repair tapes, one of which I commend to your attention. "Barrier tape," is a new generation, reinforced nylon tape that is waterproof, lightweight, and almost impossible to hole or tear. Most important, its highly aggressive self-adhesive backing sticks to anything. Available in strips or bulky rolls, Barrier tape is available at most outdoor stores or by mail from CLG Enterprises, 3838 Dight Ave. So., Minneapolis, MN 55406.

If you don't have sophisticated tape, try bandaids. Except for the aforementioned "Barrier tape," nothing sticks to nylon better than the sticky wings of a bandaid, which remain glued to the fabric through repeated washings.

TENTS

Top-of-the-line mountaineering tents cost upwards of 500 dollars today. And thousand dollar tents may be commonplace in a few years. At these prices, it pays to battle head-on the culprits which reduce longevity. Abrasion is the main enemy of tent fabrics, so careful washing—especially the outside floor and fly—after each trip is essential. Tent makers suggest that you use only mild soaps, not harsh detergents, on tent fabrics, but I disagree. The minimal damage to waterproof coatings which results from using detergents is more than offset by the amount of ground-in dirt they remove. Many outfitters machine wash their nylon tents with laundry detergent (cold water, gentle cycle) each year. How else could they keep these old tents looking like new?

Caution: close zippers and remove lines before you wash your tent. The delicate nature of nylon tents suggests they should never be washed in a top-loading machine.

Every few seasons I re-coat the seams on my tent with Thompson's Water Seal—an industrial strength chemical used for sealing wood and concrete block. Every hardware store has it.

Nylon degrades badly in the sun so don't forget to re-place your parachute cord tent lines every few years.

To separate stuck aluminum tent poles, briefly heat the joint of the larger (outside) pole with the flame of your liquid fuel stove. The pole will expand enough to permit easy removal. Afterwards, polish the joint with fine sandpaper and lubricate it with oil or WD-40.

Storage: You've probably heard that nylon tents, unlike canvas ones, won't rot if put away wet. Hogwash! Certain microorganisms attack the polyurethane coatings that are used to waterproof nylon. Once the coated surface of a tent or pack begins to "peel", the ball game's over. So be sure your tent is bone-dry before you pack it away. An oversize porous stuff sack is better protection than a tight-fitting waterproof one.

Tip: *don't store nylon tents or packs on the floor of a concrete basement. Dampness will spread from the concrete to the fabric and cause it to rot.*

PACKS

Packs accumulate moisture (and odors!) from the dirty, damp clothing carried inside. So wash and air dry packs after every trip. Failure to do so will result in "peeled polyurethane coatings" and uncomplimentary smells which are difficult to eliminate.

Simply wash packs inside and out with warm, soapy water (any dishwashing detergent will do) and hang them in the sun until they dry. Clean leather with saddle soap then rub in a wax-based leather preservative like "Snow Seal". Surface mold on leather straps and fittings may be easily removed by sponging with a 25 percent solution of bleach in water.

You can restore areas of sun-bleached canvas by painting on canvas waterproofing compounds or "Thompson's Water Seal", which may also be used to preserve maps, journals and clothing. Nylon fabrics which have lost their waterproofing may be repaired by flowing on Kenyon Industries "Re-Coat", which you can buy at most camp shops.

Packs are best stored on wooden dowels which are hung from the ceiling. Remember, polyurethane coatings will mildew if nylon packs are put away wet or are stored

Figure 5-2

in a damp area. Your storage method should provide for plenty of ventilation.

You can extend the life of a packsack by installing a double bottom—a job easily done by your shoemaker. And you can make wear-prone pack edges and stitching (and boot tips and heel counters!) abrasion-proof by coating these areas with epoxy resin.

Tip: *epoxy is as useful at home as in the field. Just about anything can be repaired with the honey colored stuff. Case in* *point: some years ago, I accidently cracked the bathroom stool with a misdirected blow from my claw hammer. Rather than junk the porcelain fixture, I applied epoxy and fiberglass cloth to the break. Fifteen years have passed and there is no sign of a leak.*

Many packs have closing flaps which are too short. These can be lengthened by sewing matching material to the pack flap. To avoid remounting severed fittings, cut off the flap at its midpoint and sew the extra fabric into place.

GROMMETS

At the outset, I should make it perfectly clear that I dislike grommets. They invariably bend, pull out, and/or tear material when the chips are down. The giant steel grommets used on truck tarps are a possible exception, though even here I give small quarter. Far better to replace these archaic fasteners with well sewn nylon loops, properly reinforced D-rings or Fastex™ buckles.

Machine installed grommets frequently are not set firmly enough to hold when the material is stressed. Fortunately, you can eliminate factory permissiveness with a die and firm whap of your claw hammer—a ritual I adopt whenever I get a new piece of grommeted gear. However, leave well enough alone if you don't have a fitted die: a mis-aligned hammer blow will make things worse.

Removing damaged grommets is difficult without proper tools. And installing new ones in damaged fabric makes no sense at all. More than likely, you'll have to reinforce the torn or oversized grommet hole with additional material on each side. Sew the fabric down before you punch the hole. If you eliminate this step the fabric will turn and wear when the grommet is stressed.

If you really want fail-proof grommets, just throw this advice to the winds and, as the opening paragraph of this section suggests, replace them with less archaic fasteners!

That's about it for maintenance and repair of your equipment. Hardly back-breaking drudgery, is it? Fact is, the cleaning and repair of each item brings forth pleasant memories of past trips. Scars, nicks and tears in equipment signify honest use, a reason why experienced trippers are reluctant to make repairs.

On the other hand, some campers are maintenance freaks and don't know when to quit. Even the best cared-for gear won't last forever. Products can be over-patched, over-epoxied, over-sewn. When an item in my camping closet has "had it", I remove and save useable items like buckles, straps and unworn material, and keep them for repairing other things.

There's a reverse form of snobbery which suggests that pilled, worn shirts, over-patched trousers, and worn out boot soles are the mark of an expert. Perhaps. But when you're 100 miles from the nearest road and a packstrap breaks or your tent comes apart at the seams, you'll wish you had adopted a more sensible approach. After all, it is attention to the "details" of the sport which separate winners from the almost ran.

CHAPTER

SIX

• • •

Selective Outfitting

Tucked away in a remote corner of Manitoba, is the awesomely beautiful North Knife River. It leaves North Knife Lake with a determined rush and flexes its muscles as one continuous rapid enroute to Hudson's Bay. Much of the whitewater along the way is too difficult to paddle. That which can be run often requires precise teamwork to negotiate.

Since there are no defined portages (not even animal trails), getting around dangerous rapids and falls often requires horsing canoes and gear over high rock ledges and through thick brush—a procedure which demands sweat and careful compass work.

Forty miles from the ocean's estuary, the canoeist encounters dreaded mud flats and must choose whether to camp on wet, oozing muck, or keep on paddling. There is also the danger of a polar bear encounter: in 1991, we saw eleven of them!

Finally, there is the 30 mile paddle to Churchill on Hudson's Bay. Twelve foot tides can leave an unsuspecting canoeist stranded on mud for hours at the mercy of dangerous weather and aggressive bears. Cold and unforgiving, "The Bay" is no place to capsize far from shore.

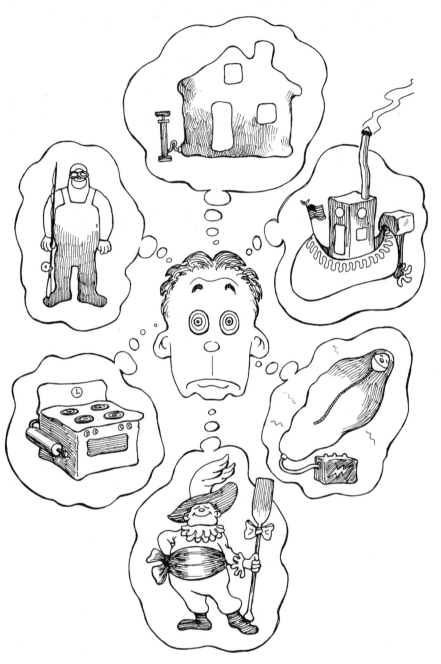

Figure 6-1

Simply put, the North Knife River is a trip for experts only. Hauntingly wild and beautiful, barely one canoe party a year answers its call. But for paddlers who have the right stuff, solitude and challenge are guaranteed.

Knowing this, I was certain we would not encounter another canoe party on the river. Imagine our chagrin when 30 miles from The Bay, we discovered an aging 17 foot Grumman perched on a small island. An elderly man waved us in and we disembarked for a chat.

His silver-gray beard and brown, weathered hands suggested he was pushing 70. Two months of strenuous outdoor living had made him lean and fit, a part of the land rather than an intruder into it. He had begun his voyage a month earlier and had already canoed the Seal River to Churchill, braving alone the icy waters of Hudson's bay. He was now returning to his starting point at Leaf Rapids alone—an incomprehensible feat that required going up the difficult river we had so cautiously come down. Were it not for my belief that nothing is impossible, I would have shouted the word. But instead, I numbly answered his questions about what lay upstream.

Then, I listened to him explain his dream. A retired welder and jack-of-all trades from Regina, Saskatchewan, he had canoed northern rivers for as long as he could remember. It was his preference to travel alone, and at 90 days, this would be his longest trip. He had little money and cared not a wit for the things that it could buy. By our standards, his equipment was archaic. Clothed head to toe in woolens, his attire was a mix of bargain basement castoffs, home-spuns, and military surplus items.

Yet, he seemed as comfortable as any of us. The rain had stopped and the man unconsciously unzipped his hoodless, tattered yellow rain coat. I followed suit, embarrassed by the crackle of my expensive Gore-tex jacket. As we talked, I sized up his outfit: the big Grumman canoe was way too much boat for a man to handle alone, especially on an upstream run. He had three cheap spruce paddles which were too long, too heavy, and too flimsy for a trip of this magnitude. Proudly, he showed us the "closet pole" he would use to propel his canoe back upstream to Leaf Rapids. Not an ash or aluminum river pole, mind you, but a standard Douglas fir closet pole!

Snuggled against a screen of trees on a gentle hummock, was his little Eureka timberline tent. It was factory stock, without vestibule or expedition grade poles. An interior plastic groundsheet and two nylon storm-lines kept it dry and taut in the persistent wind and rain.

With cold-numbed fingers that protruded from fingerless wool gloves (the kind that trout fishermen wear), he reached into the breast pocket of his wool mackinaw and withdrew a teabag. As he poured hot water, he remarked that he was out of sugar; but no matter, "I'll learn to like it that way." We had plenty so I gave him two cups. He nodded an unemotional thanks.

As we paddled away, I glanced back and wondered if his stoic confidence belied incompetence or expertise. By my standards, his gear was out of synch for the rigors at hand, yet his demeanor and accomplishments suggested otherwise. In my writings, I have always made a fetish for the value of knowledge over things. Nonetheless, I knew this man was undergunned, for I had just traversed with the best of gear what for him still lay ahead.

A warm feeling grew upwards from the pit of my stomach and surfaced as a grin. Somehow, I knew the old gentleman would make it—drained and tired perhaps, but he'd make it. Later that fall, I learned he had reached Leaf Rapids without incident. And right on schedule to boot!

Thousands of miles away at a different time, a similar scenario was in progress. A father and son were making their third arctic canoe trip when the weather turned sour. The hooded cotton sweatshirts and leather boots they wore provided inadequate protection from the chilling rain. When an arctic gale, with its 50 mile per hour winds sliced across the tundra, they holed up in their discount store tent and huddled together for warmth.

Then suddenly, a metal connecting tube in the tent gave way and the structure collapsed—a repeat of an experience on an earlier trip. The replacement part was "guaranteed" not to fail—a matter the father would look into when they got home. Remarkably, the two survived the storm, only to make navigational errors and run out of food.

So miserable and desperate were these two that they swore an oath to God (they placed a note in a rock cairn!) that they would never return to the barren lands in return for safe passage home.

Fortunately, the two returned home safely and have since renegged on their promise. They've made other successful arctic canoe trips, but with new insight and better equipment.

How are these events related? In both cases, there was improper or questionable equipment, fierce stubbornness and pride. But, his wool attire, heavy rain coat and attention to detail—as in the choice of location and method of storm-proofing his tent—suggested that the old man knew what he was doing. Aware of the limits of his gear, he adopted a careful pace, camped in protected places, and did not use his delicate pole in powerful currents. He had no money for polypropylene and pile so he substituted time-tested wool. When we parted, it was 45°, lightly raining, and the wind was blowing fairly well. The wave and solemn smile he flashed me as I eddied out suggested he was as comfortable as me.

On the other hand, the father and son were cheechakos in a foreign land—and were in fact, so unfamiliar with its requirements that they didn't have the foggiest idea of what (equipment and food) was needed to survive. No wonder they continually exceeded the limits of their gear and time and again got into trouble! As evidenced by their poor planning—they broke the same tent pole and nearly ran out of food on a previous trip—they didn't learn from past experiences. With four "successful" arctic trips under their belt, they should have known better. They had the earmarks of experts, but were really bumbling idiots whose thoughtlessness and inattention to detail on two occasions nearly cost them their lives.

Their accomplishments are noteworthy only because their bodies were able to tolerate the abuse to which they were constantly subjected. Better gear alone would not have solved their problems. What this pair needed was common sense and backwoods know how!

Okay, if good skills and mediocre equipment can usually save the day, why invest in first class gear? There are many reasons, though heading the list is usually "pride of ownership." For more often than not, functional differences that separate "good" from "great" are often so slight that they will be appreciated only by the most experienced users under the most demanding conditions.

For example, witness the number of people who buy sophisticated home computers, then use them to run games and low memory word-processing programs. Ditto for $400 storm suits which earn their pay only when the wearers get caught in the rain while walking from the parking lot to the office.

Of course, the dangerous antithesis is that if you're going in harm's way where equipment failure can be serious, overkill makes sense, even if you don't think you can afford it. The problem is matching your needs to the demands of your environment.

Case in point: Some years ago, I evaluated compasses for a major magazine and rated the military proven Suunto KB-14, "most accurate." The Suunto could be consistently read to within 15 minutes (one quarter degree) of arc of a test theodolite. Nothing could match its performance.

As soon as my article appeared, the owner of a local equipment shop called to say there had been a run on KB-14's and 20's (a lower priced version of the same compass). He reported that people were buying them for "canoeing the Boundary Waters"—an activity for which these instruments were ill suited. When he tried to steer them towards less accurate but more versatile orienteering compasses, they were adamant. "The customer is always right," he said, and what the customer wanted was the top-rated compass, even if a protractor and pencil—and some math—were needed to figure map bearings and declination.

Not all equipment errors are the result of inexperience. Even the pros occasionally goof up. For example, consider the case of the scoutmaster who for years had relied on Redwing hunting boots for summer hiking in Minnesota.

When the man was invited to co-lead a backpacking trip in Isle Royale National Park, he jumped at the chance. "Better get some real hiking boots," advised the senior leader. "Those Redwings won't stand up to the tough hiking we'll do."

So like a good citizen, the scoutmaster set out in search of "more serious" boots. The young store clerk he collared told him that conditions on Isle Royale were enough similar to that in Minnesota that his old faithful Redwings would do fine—good advice which the scoutmaster promptly ignored.

Instead, he asked to see the store's top-rated hiking boot which, at nearly four pounds, looked sturdy enough for jumping out of airplanes! But wouldn't it be too hot and stiff for summer hiking in an evergreen forest? And would the thick padding ever dry out if he stepped in swamp water over his ankles? He also wondered if the cleated lugs which gripped so well on dry boulders would provide good traction on damp spruce needles and wet rock. Surely, they would load up with mud after the first rain. But the man put aside these concerns and confidently wrote out a check. After all, a major magazine, and the store clerk, had said these were best. So what if they were stiff and heavy and looked awkward. He'd learned it paid to keep an open mind: surely, the new boots would perform flawlessly once they were broken in.

You know the rest of the story: the "top rated" hikers performed as the scoutmaster feared. He kept a tight lip throughout the trip then afterwards quietly sold them at a garage sale.

So how did these boots receive a top rating if they performed so badly in the field? Simple: they were evaluated in dry mountainous terrain, not in relatively flat evergreen forest where it rains all the time. The thick-soled boots provided great support and traction on the steep talus slopes—an activity that would have shred the scoutmaster's beloved Redwing's the first day out. But there's a big difference between woodland trail hiking and scrambling up boulder scree. The scoutmaster knew the difference and he should have stuck to what "his own experience" had taught him was best for the job!

It's beyond the scope of this book to detail the specifics of equipment design and construction. If you want comparative data, check out any modern backpacking or canoeing book. Or, read the monthly product tests which appear in outdoor specialty magazines. *Backpacker, Canoe, Outside* and other sport publications publish an annual index which lists specific gear items and the issue in which they were evaluated. Your local librarian will help you locate this information.

So rather than bore you with equipment facts which you can easily find elsewhere, I'll share with you a philosophy which works for me. Follow these guidelines before you hand over your VISA card, and you won't get burned when you select equipment:

1. As the anecdotes suggest, what works best in one environment may be poorly adapted to another, so thoroughly research the area in which you plan to travel before you commit to specific things. If you're fanatic about a discipline (like mountain climbing or desert hiking) to the exclusion of everything else, consider specialized items that will give you an edge. Otherwise, select more versatile, "sedan-rated" equipment.

2. Disregard entirely the advice of "experts" who have not repeatedly walked in your moccasins. Don't make the same mistake as the scoutmaster who gave up his Redwing boots!

3. Don't take magazine product tests too seriously. Writers work on deadline and are usually paid by the length of copy they produce not the time they spend researching and field-testing. Time is money, so research and product testing are kept to a minimum. Bad reviews often mean losing advertisers, which are a magazine's life blood.

4. Keep competitive gear in its place. Whitewater slalom canoeing, technical mountain climbing and triathlon are not at all like the rigors of serious wilderness travel. More often than not, what works best in competition is awkward or dangerous afield.

Best advice I can give you when choosing equipment is to carefully examine everything before you buy. If a zipper looks weak, it probably is; if there's a knob which can break, it probably will; if there's a loose part than can be lost, bet on it. Go on the assumption that if something can fail, it will, and you'll get real value for your money and be well prepared for the unexpected.

Most important, be aware that some of the most highly touted products which work flawlessly over the short haul, fail miserably when the weeks turn to years. So be wary of advertising claims and the testimonials of individuals whose experience is limited to a single expedition. Instead, heed the advice of those who travel wild places year after year. These are the real experts, even though their opinions are seldom seen in print.

Enough philosophy. Here are some suggestions along with expert advice.

FOOTWEAR

The rule is supple leather or fabric topped boots for serious backpacking, shoe-pacs (leather tops and rubber bottoms) for sloppy spring hiking and three-season canoeing, knee-high rubber boots for mud slogging and wading icy streams, and felt-lined mukluks or Canadian Sorels™ for extreme cold. Adopt what local foresters, wildlife managers and other outdoor professionals wear and you won't go wrong.

Boots should always be worn with two pairs of socks—a thin, polpropylene or pure wool liner next to the skin, and a thick, nearly pure wool over-sock. Wear the liner sock inside-out to prevent seams from chafing your skin. Socks should come above the tops of your boots so they won't slide down and bunch up as you walk. You can wear expensive high socks to keep your legs warm or simply put on long johns.

Stiff-sided, thick-soled boots that restrict ankle movement are for mountaineering not hiking. The best "trail boots" have flexible soles, ankle-high unpadded uppers (padding absorbs and holds water) and weigh as little as possible. Some boots have high backs that slope forward or tight-fitting elastic "scree" collars at the ankle to keep out stones and twigs. However, collars and protuberances that are tight enough to eliminate debris restrict circulation and pinch the achilles tendon as you walk. The result is painful tendonitis!

Except for boulder scrambling where you need thick padding,[1] the trend is to lightweight non-agressive soles which are kind to your feet and the environment. And speaking of weight, the U.S. army has determined that one pound on your feet is equivalent to five pounds on your back. Pedal your bike once around the block while wearing four pound hiking boots then switch to running shoes and you'll discover the true meaning of "light-of-foot".

How to size your boots: wear proper socks and slide your feet as far forward as possible in your unlaced boots. Stand erect so that both boots are equally weighted. If you feel pressure aginst the sides of your feet, the boot is too narrow. Now, lace each boot comfortably and take a walk: your heel should not rise and your feet should not slide forward and

---

[1]The more you weigh, the more padding you need beneath your feet. A 300 pound hiker (weight of person plus pack) requires a thicker sole than a 200 pound hiker.

touch the end of the boot when you firmly kick a hard object. There are subtle differences between American and European feet, so some "properly sized" foreign made boots may not provide a good fit for everyone. As every soldier will attest, combat boots made on the official Munson last are the most comfortable boots of all. Too bad all American boot makers don't follow this proven pattern.

Tip: *if you have hard-to-fit feet with narrow heels that "lift" with every step you take, ask your shoe repair person to glue a thin leather heel cup and riser inside your boot. One manufacturer, L.L. Bean, receives so many requests for this service that they offer it as an option.*

Insoles: Removeable insoles are a welcome addition to any boot. Those made of leather, sheepskin and other porous materials that will absorb perspiration, are cooler and more comfortable than rubber or plastic ones that don't breathe. Buy boots a half size larger to make room for insoles.

Insoles add considerable warmth in sub-freezing temperatures. Again, those made of thick wool felt or natural sheepskin are best. If you need more insulation, place one-eighth inch thick mesh insoles (you can make them from nylon or steel screen) beneath your wool insoles. The mesh will trap perspiration that would otherwise be retained by your socks. Closed-cell (non-porous) foam insoles are best placed next to the boot sole. A thin piece of closed cell foam placed under the heel is often enough to keep cold from seeping in when you stand on ice.

In summary, stack insulation from the boot sole up as follows: 1) Closed-cell foam or mesh insole, 2) wool felt liner ("snowmobile boot liner"), 3) wool felt or sheepskin insole, 4) duffel or wool ragg sock, 5) polypropylene or wool liner sock.

Serious winter boots should be purchased at least two sizes larger than street shoes to make room for felt liners and insoles and the heavy socks you'll wear inside. Be sure to break in your boots before your trip or you may suffer unpleasant consequences, as this anecdote reveals:

On Breaking in Boots

by Sue Harings

Sue Harings is a Home Economics/Quest teacher from River Falls, Wisconsin, who has hiked, scuba-dived, and canoed in some of the most remote regions of the world. Sue has canoed, hiked, and winter camped (at temperatures to 40 below) alone, and has paddled Great Slave Lake, the Churchill and Hood Rivers in northern Canada.

"My first backpacking trip was on Baffen Island, up Pangnirtung Pass, in 1989. I was 43 at the time, hardly a teenager. My hiking boots were purchased new in Brussels, Belgium in 1975, but had not been worn until this trip. Brand names aside, they are typical mid-seventies, ankle-high, hiking boots. With Vibram lugged soles and classic scree shield, they weigh about 3-1/2 pounds, which is very heavy by today's standards.

I learned the hard way that it pays to break in your boots well before a trip, and to wear the right socks. It was assumed that if you were ready to tackle Baffin Island, you knew what to wear on your feet. Not me. Instead of the customary two pairs of socks, I wore just one pair of heavy wool socks inside my stiff hiking boots. First day out I wore the skin right off my heels. That night, I applied moleskin (Spenco™ Second Skin is much better) to the injury but that wasn't enough. Within days, I lost my big toe nail and bruised the top of all my toes. At this point, the pain was unbearable and I couldn't continue, so I hung the boots over my pack frame and put on my Saucony™ tennies. Ahhhh, instant relief! I wore the Sauconies the rest of the trip without incident, even while climbing steep glacial moraine.

On a later trip in Glacier National Park, I wore the same boots, this time, well broken in and with proper socks, without problems. They were ideal for scree hiking but were not very comfortable on blistering hot days. At these times, I wore two pairs of socks inside my Alp Sport river sandals, and these worked fine, even with a 60 pound Kelty frame pack. Later, I learned that contrary to popular belief, sandals are not outlandish hiking shoes—many Sherpas wear them while toting heavy loads in the Himalayas.

I believe that having several kinds of "hiking footwear" (boots, sandals, running shoes), and switching them each day (or as conditions warrant), prevents foot problems on a long hike. However, my short, wide feet don't fit standard shoe sizes very well. At any rate, this procedure works for me.

Some go-light purists may question carrying boots, tennies, and sandals. But you need an extra pair of shoes for camp anyway. And my sandals weigh less than a pound—hardly enough to get hyper over.

Equally important as good shoes, is a strong hiking staff which comes in handy for traversing tricky spots like boulders and streams. A staff helps maintain balance, especially when going downhill while carrying a heavy backpack. I can't say enough good things about my hiking staff, which provides good traction on snow and ice (it has a convertible rubber/steel tip) and doubles as a camera monopod."

CLOTHING

There's cotton, wool, polypropylene, polyester pile, nylon and a host of high-tech blends. You can make a good case for every one, even cotton which, on hot, humid days, is the most comfortable fabric of all. The key, of course, is to dress in layers—one thin fabric over another—so that the heat you produce will warm your body not the environment.

Every material has its warriors who will rally to support it, though what's best depends largely on your pocketbook, perspective and local availability. Polyester pile, for example, is luxuriously soft and warm and it dries quickly after a rainstorm. But the fabric pills, is bulky, has a narrow temperature comfort range and is neither windproof nor water-repellent.

Polypropylene—a popular fabric for long underwear—absorbs no moisture, but it retains and magnifies body odors (the stuff smells downright awful after a few days!), is dissolved by the solvents in some insecticides and loses thermal efficiency as it becomes loaded with body oils and dirt. Polypro also melts at low temperature which means you can't place it in a hot clothes drier. A campfire spark means a certain hole, and a nasty burn—something the British navy discovered when sailors who wore it were burned alive on their ships during the short Argentine war.

Nylon is more windproof and less sensitive to chemicals than polypropylene, but it is also dangerous around open flame. Tightly woven wool is more wind and water repellent than pile and it is not affected by solvents, oils or dirt. Air drying in sunlight is all that's needed to eliminate most odors.

However, wet wool is heavy when dry, still heavier when wet, and it dries slowly if it becomes thoroughly soaked. But wear pile in a cold, all day rain and see if you prefer it to wool. Admittedly, if you remove the pile garment and twirl it about your head to spin off accumulated moisture, then put it on again, it will edge out wool in warmth, light weight and comfort. But, if the weave fills with frigid water, the contest may take a different twist as your skin cools from evaporative heat loss. Wool, as every aficionado will attest, dries from the skin out—a characteristic which usually defies chilling.

However, clever use of synthetics negates their disadvantages and synergizes their good points. For example, polypropylene or polyester underwear wicks moisture to wool and pile outerwear where it evaporates without cooling your skin—a feature you'll appreciate if you work up a sweat on a chilly day. Add a nylon shell and you'll stop wind in its tracks. Wear a waterproof garment over all these clothes and you'll stay warm and dry in any weather.

For canoeing, synthetics which can be spun dry with a twist of the wrist have the edge over wool. Except for socks, hats, mittens and trousers, ditto for winter wear, as you'll read below:

How to Choose Cold Weather Clothing

by Al Gustaveson

Al Gustaveson has served as president of the Minnesota Canoe Association and is a past program director for Wilderness Inquiry, a nationally known outdoor adventure travel group. He has led wilderness trips in Ontario, Manitoba and the Northwest Territories, and has paddled thousands of miles in wood-strip canoes he has built himself. Al is an experienced guide who enjoys the outdoors (and the poems of Robert Service!) in every season.

"Growing up in Minnesota presupposes that one automatically knows how to dress for cold weather. Not true. Not only is the learning curve still in effect but the materials to learn about have changed drastically too. Gone are the sheepskin coats, four buckle rubber overshoes, cotton union suits and army surplus, white-painted, wooden skis that made us feel like Finnish resistance fighters on the 1939 Russian front.

The new fabrics and materials today make winter much more enjoyable. The key is in layering your clothing so that you have a number of combinations to suit changing temperatures and conditions. The new plastic fabrics are much lighter and warmer than the cottons and flannels of my youth, and they're reasonably priced. Almost every discount house now has serviceable polypropylene and pile garments in stock to fit budget-minded shoppers. Nylon, or other synthetic wind-shells and pants, Holofil™ parkas and polypro socks, are available and will extend the range of outdoor activities. Wool shirts and surplus heavy duty army pants are about the only items from the old days that still make a fine addition to your "layered look".

Sorels™ and snowmobile boots have replaced the cold rubber boots of yore. When worn correctly, with layered socks of lightweight polypropylene, and wool socks over them, feet stay warm to subzero temperatures. For serious outdoors people, mukluks, the native footwear of the far north, are a worthwhile investment. Finding a pair can be a challenge[2], but once you have worn them in really cold weather, their advantages become obvious. The secret is the soft non-heat transferring soles of the mukluk as compared to the hard, heat robbing soles of regular boots. Worn large, with felt liners and extra felt insoles, layered socks of polypro and wool, mukluks are the warmest way to save your toes from discomfort.

Once you have all the stuff the trick is in the way you put it together. Start with a polypro turtleneck and long john bottoms. Cover these with your heavy wool pants and shirt, and add a pile sweater. Next comes tightly woven wind pants and a windproof anorak parka or top with a hood. Use Dacron, acrylic or wool "wristlets" under your "choppers" (wool mittens worn inside deerskin mitten shells) and be sure to wear knee-high gaiters if you're venturing into deep snow. Top this with a pure wool Navy watch cap and an ear

---

[2]Traditional moosehide mukluks, like the ones Will Steger wore on his Antarctica expedition, are available from Steger Mukluks, 125 North Central Ave., Ely, MN 55731. Phone: 1-800-543-0773. U.S. and Canadian army mukluks are sometimes available in military surplus stores (CJ).

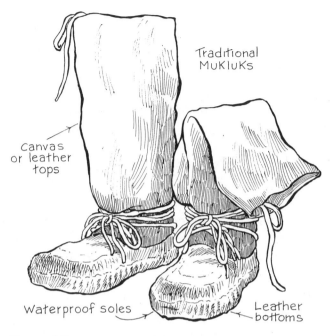

Traditional
MukluKs

Canvas
or leather
tops

Waterproof soles

Leather
bottoms

Figure 6-2

band to cover your nose, and you're ready for almost anything.

After you put your system together the learning curve kicks in when you discover how to take it off. Keeping dry is the key. Dry is warm; wet is cold. Polypropylene works so well because it does not absorb and hold water next to your skin and rob your body of heat. Knowing that, you'll want to stay as dry as you can. Don't overheat by wearing too many layers during active periods. Learn to keep warm by adding or removing layers of clothing before you get too hot or cold.

Yesterday's fabrics don't measure up to today's new, warm stuff. Shop for your cold weather system carefully. Add what you need when it goes on sale (e.g., buy long johns and wool hats in spring) and you'll be ready for next winter's fun, without spending a lot of money."

Bill Forgey

Few are more knowledgeable about cold weather gear than Dr. Bill Forgey, whose highly acclaimed books *Wilderness Medicine* and *Hypothermia* are the acknowledged resources in the field. When he's not doctoring patients at his clinic in Merrillville, Indiana, Dr. Forgey is traveling the wilds of northern Canada. Two decades ago, "Doc" built a log cabin—the one in which Scott Power and David Scott over-wintered—in a remote corner of northern Manitoba. Forgey combines modern technology with the proven ways of Calvin Rutstrum (whose book *Paradise Below Zero* makes great reading) to enjoy sustained outdoor living in temperatures to 50 below. Says Dr. Forgey:

"My winter outfit has undergone a considerable change during the past several years. I am a strong supporter of using a vapor barrier liner in my boots and sleeping bag for temperatures below zero degrees Fahrenheit. Its major aid is in the prevention of moisture build up in boot liners or in the bag insulation. My favorite winter boots are duffel lined Canadian Armed Forces mukluks (available through surplus store outlets in Canada) or Steger designed mukluks with the Canadian surplus duffel liners, not the felt liners that Steger now produces.

I use a layer system, consisting of medium or heavy polypropylene underwear tops and bottoms, wool shirt or Polartec™ 300 top, heavy weight (30 oz) wool pants (generally available from L.L. Bean), an over-sized baffled down, hooded parka and a wool lined outer parka in triple extra large size, also hooded. One of the hoods should have a fur ruff to form a snorkel for re-breathing. Fur is necessary so that the frost can be easily knocked off.

I use either down expedition mittens (Eddie Bauer or REI) or heavy weight wool mittens with an over-mitt. I carry a face mask and a balaclava style wool-polypro hat.

"I do not feel that Gore-Tex™ or other waterproof/breathable outerwear makes much sense for below zero use, but I swear by the stuff during light freeze and above freezing temperatures."

Deb Erdmann

Deb Erdmann, winter program director for Camp Voyageur, P.O. Box 420, Ely, Minnesota 55731, offers some important advice about choosing cold weather footwear. Camp Voyageur offers an all season sports, athletics and wilderness tripping program for boys and girls in the Boundary Waters Canoe Area, Quetico Provincial Park and Isle Royale National Park. Their unique winter program encourages individuals and groups to explore the north country by cross-country ski and dog sled.

"Warm boots are the single most important piece of equipment you need to make a safe, enjoyable winter camping trip. In northern Minnesota we typically use shoe-pacs with removeable felt or synthetic liners such as Sorel™, Timberland™, LaCrosse™ and Red Ball™. Some people prefer traditional mukluks with the same kind of removeable liners. The important thing is to size boots big enough so they'll fit comfortably over two pairs of socks and the boot liner. You should be able to wiggle your toes easily. Correctly sized boots trap dead air which acts as an insulator. Boots that are too small do not allow sufficient room for toes to move and generate heat.

Always carry at least three changes of socks and an extra pair of boot liners. Wear one pair of liners and socks during the day and change to the second set when you crawl into your sleeping bag. A third set of liners and socks provide a backup if something gets wet.

Begin the day with a dry pair of polypropylene, Thermax™ or silk liner socks and a pair of thick wool oversocks. Never wear cotton socks! Removeable boot liners may be made from synthetics such as polyester fleece, Polar plus™ or wool felt. Wear a gaiter or wind shell pant over your boots to keep snow from getting in.

Your feet will get damp as you ski and hike, but this should cause little discomfort if temperatures stay above zero and you are relatively active. Simply change to dry socks and liners when you reach camp at the end of the day and use a warming fire to dry out damp liners and socks. You can further dry boot liners and socks by taking them into your sleeping bag when you retire. Your boots will be much easier to put on the morning if you open the tops as wide as you can before you go to bed.

If winter camping becomes a favorite pastime, you may want to invest in a second pair of boots or mukluks to wear in camp. It's a luxury to change into dry boots after wearing damp pack boots all day. Here are some do's and don'ts to remember:

Do's

1. Size boots BIG.
2. Take at least three pairs of liner socks and three pairs of thick insulating socks.
3. Take at least one spare pair of boot liners.
4. Wear synthetic or wool blend socks.
5. Wear gaiters or wind pant bottoms over the tops of your boots.

6. Take time to dry all damp items around the fire at night.

7. Open your boots as wide as possible before going to sleep.

Don'ts

1. Don't wear boots that are too small!

2. Don't wear cotton socks!

3. Don't wear damp socks to bed at night!"

Sandy Bridges

Few know more about cold feet than Sandy Bridges who, since 1970, has been the director of Sommers Canoe Base (Northern Tier National High Adventure center) near Ely, Minnesota. "Sommers" is internationally known for its innovative—and safe!—outdoor experiences. When winter comes to northern Minnesota, thoughts turn from canoeing to winter camping, in temperatures to 30 below! Under Bridge's expert direction, winter gear and methods are tested and revised. The innovative use of inexpensive open-celled foam for cold weather sleeping bags and clothing is one example of how seriously scouters take the sport of winter camping. Says Sandy Bridges:

"When anyone talks of cold, the first thing that I think of is 'cold feet'. If your feet are cold your entire body will suffer. The old adages about warming your feet, such as: feet cold—eat something, exercise, put on a hat—will all work, but only if you have proper footwear that fits well and is adequately insulated.

Winter, or snow camping, is relatively new. Yes, you can find books on the subject that date back to the late 1800's. The Boy Scouts of America even printed a handbook on the subject in 1927. The truth though, is that until a very few years ago only a handful of people really went winter snow camping. The small numbers involved did not impress the people that make cold weather equipment and so most of what you could buy was designed for ice fishing and snowmobiling. Day trips on skis have been more popular and this sport is the one self-propelled winter activity that equipment-wise has not been "left out in the cold".

The KEY to staying WARM is the word C-O-L-D:

- Keep yourself, clothing and equipment CLEAN
- Avoid OVERHEATING
- Wear clothing, LOOSE, LIGHTWEIGHT, LONG and in LAYERS
- Keep DRY at all costs (this is especially important for footwear)

One excellent method for keeping your feet warm is to use open-celled polyurethane foam insulation inside your boots. The late Gil Phillips, known by the Boy Scouts as the "Foam Man" perfected the use of poly foam for clothing and footwear. The system that Gil developed is described and recommended in the current B.S.A. FIELDBOOK. Poly foam is an ideal insulator because it:

- meets all the requirements for the "Key to Staying Warm".
- is easy to clean
- prevents overheating by "pumping" air into the boot as you walk.
- moves air away from the feet and keeps them dry.

- Poly foam must be worn loose: Gil always said that poly foam was a "micro layer" material (a series of layers bonded together).

What we wear on our feet depends largely on the "type" of cold we will experience.

WET COLD: +50°F down to +14°F.

DRY COLD: +14°F down to −20°F.

ARCTIC LIKE COLD: Minus 20°F and below.

For temperatures below 14°F (DRY COLD and ARCTIC LIKE COLD) we recommend a good quality, lightweight outer boot that is not insulated. A mukluk works great. Just be sure that the insulation is not sewn into the boot. You should wear the following inside your boots:

- One or two 3/8-1/2 inch thick, closed-cell foam insoles.
- A one inch thick polyurethane foam "foot wrap" (the Boy Scout FIELDBOOK and BSA OKPIK HANDBOOK has plans for making these foot wraps), or a foam bootie.
- A pair of "wicking" (polypropylene, Thermax™ or light wool) socks next to the foot.

For WET COLD temperatures we use the same materials but sometimes modify them as follows:

- Waterproof boots, such as four or five buckle overshoes. These must be large enough to cover your foot, insoles and poly foam insulation.
- Plastic socks (plastic bag or other vapor barrier liner) between the boot and insulation keeps

the insulation from getting wet from the outside[3].

- Plastic socks between the liner socks and insulation keeps insulation dry and prevents outside moisture from getting to the feet. Be sure to check your feet regularly if you wear plastic bags (vapor barrier liners) inside your boots.

Common sense suggests that you should...

- check your feet several times a day and massage them as necessary.
- dry wash your feet each day with a good brand of moisture absorbing (high content of aluminum chlorohydrate) foot powder.
- change liner socks each day or when they become damp.
- dry footwear at every opportunity.
- carry two pairs of boots—one designed for trail use and one or more for wearing in camp. Camp footwear may require more insulation since you are less active."

THE ALL IMPORTANT TENT

Your comfort and safety depends upon your tent, so don't buy the first good deal that comes along. Each person needs about 2-1/2 by 7 feet just to stretch out. Add an additional half foot (3' × 7') plus headroom enough to dress, and you

---

[3]Sandy says that vapor barrier liners placed next to the skin, as recommended in winter camping texts, don't work well for inexperienced scouts who don't follow directions very well. The "modified" vapor barrier method suggested here makes for drier and warmer feet. Scouts are admonished to change liner socks as soon as they become damp. Bridges prefers the heavy plastic socks which are used as foot and boot covers in the food industry.

Figure 6-3

enter the realm of comfort. For backpacking, figure on a maximum weight of 3 pounds per person.

You'll pay much more for high-tech geometrics—domes, tunnels and such—than for simple-to-sew but reliable A-frame designs. And be aware that price does not necessarily indicate foul weather performance or ease-of-pitching. In fact, some of the most weatherproof and windstable tents cost less than some of the worst. A superior three-season backcountry tent will have many of these features:

1. A waterproof rainfly that stakes right to the ground, or nearly so. The fly covers every seam and zipper.

2. There are no perimeter seams (which can leak) at ground level. Instead, the floor is sewn to the canopy several inches above ground. This "bathtub" construction keeps flowing ground water from seeping into the tent.

3. Generously sized awnings cover doorways and windows.

4. Poles are tempered, shock-corded aluminum. There's no such thing as a good fiberglass pole!

5. The fabric rigs drum-tight when the tent is pitched. There are extra storm loops on the fly face and hem to stabilize the tent in high winds.

6. The insect screen is outside the door panel so you can ventilate the tent without letting in bugs.

7. There is a built-in or add-on floorless vestibule (alcove) at one or both ends. Vestibules stormproof the ends of a tent and provide a place to store wet gear.

WINTER TENTS

Turn-of-the-century winter tents were either commodious canvas affairs (Baker and Forester designs) whose fronts opened to face a cheery fire, or tight, conical designs (like the famed "Miner"[4]) which were rigged to accept a sheet-metal stove. Todays hikers scoff at stove-warmed tents thinking they are too heavy and bulky for self-propelled wilderness travel. But a two person cotton tent and stove may weigh under 20 pounds, which is not too heavy to pack

---

[4]You can get modern and period canvas tentage from TENT-SMITHS, Box 496, North Conway, NH 03860. Cabela's, Inc., 812-13th Ave., Sidney, NE 69160, offers the "Alaknak™" tent (a modern version of the Miner's tent) which is designed for stove use. Cabela's Alaknak folding sheepherder's stove weighs 8 pounds, including a stove pipe with 45 degree elbow.

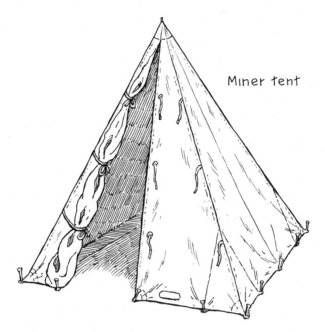

Miner tent

Figure 6-4

on a toboggan or fiberglass pulk. Dr. Bill Forgey, who winter camps in northern Manitoba for weeks at a time, prefers the double-walled canvas tent and stove to conventional nylon shelters. Says Dr. Forgey:

"For sub-zero camping, a double wall canvas tent is the next best thing to a snow cave or quinzee hut. I have modified an old Eureka Drawtite canvas tent with a full canvas fly cover and rigged it with a kerosine stove with a stove pipe out a front panel. While arctic canvas tents can be made, they are not readily obtainable. Consequently, much of our winter travel has been done with double wall, free standing nylon tents, relying on intermittent use of a Peak1 trail stove for cooking and some warmth. This stove must be lit outside the tent or a flash fire may result and cause serious burns.

We calculate a need for one quart of Coleman fuel per day of sub-zero camping, primarily for food and water preparation and to concurrently provide a modest amount of warmth."

Caution: safety demands that a stove equipped tent be constructed from a porous, flame resistant fabric, like cotton. As the following anecdote by Scott Power reveals, you should never substitute aluminum foil for proper flame-proof thimbles and stove pipe extensions.

"It was 40 below zero on January 30, 1991, in northern Manitoba. David Scott and I were in dire need of food and water after a grueling hike. We proceeded to set up our double-wall canvas tent, which was heated by a portable kerosine stove and pipe system. But as I was installing the stove, I realized that one small piece of pipe was missing. Without it, there would be no fire and escape from the minus 40 cold. So in desperation, I made a structure out of aluminum foil to compensate for the missing part. It worked. Temporarily.

About the same time the ice and snow was melting to drink for water, I noticed black smoke in the tent. I looked up and saw the tent ceiling and door was on fire. Without hesitation, I put on a pair of fire gloves to grab the hot stove and toss it outside the tent into the snow. Then, I began to extinguish the flames with snow. Almost as soon as it started, the fire was out. And we had a new window in our tent we didn't want."

You'll find more information about tent design and construction, along with practical stormproofing procedures and ideas for building your own tent, in my book, *The Basic Essentials of Trailside Shelters*, published by ICS Books.

SLEEPING BAGS

Most people buy sleeping bags that are too warm. For summer use, a reasonably confining bag filled with one and one-half pounds of high quality goose down or two pounds of Polarguard™ or Quallofil™, is ideal. Bags with more insulation than this are apt to be too hot in temperatures above 50 degrees Fahrenheit.

Down is lighter, more compact and has a wider temperature comfort range than any of the synthetics. It is also far more durable. For example, a heavily used polyester filled sleeping bag may last 8 to 10 years, while an equivalently built down bag may be serviceable for 20 or 30 years. In all likelihood, the nylon shell of a down bag will wear out long before the down.

Bags filled with down are also more luxurious to sleep in than those filled with other materials. If you've ever slept on a feather bed or beneath a down comforter you know what I mean. When wet, however, the high tech polyesters outperform down by a wide margin—the reason why they are the hands down choice for cold and rainy weather.

Winter bags should be larger (more loosely fitting) than summer bags so you'll have room to dress inside. Minus 40 degree Fahrenheit sleeping bags are available for cold weather die hards at premium prices, but a more versatile and equally warm option is to simply nest a lightweight summer bag inside a three-season one. Here's Dr. Forgey's solution to cold weather comfort:

"To sleep well in sub-zero temperatures it is critical to have adequate ground insulation. Generally, we accomplish this by using several foam pads. This insulation must be protected from body condensation and frost melt by either using close-celled systems or by covering open-celled foam with waterproof material.

I use a heavy outer sleeping bag, lined with a thin inner bag. The inner bag drapes around my neck and shoulders to prevent a "bellows effect" sucking cold air onto the sleeper (an alternative is to drape a wool sweater over your chest and shoulders: CJ). I always use a vapor barrier liner to prevent my sleeping bags from becoming damp, thus keeping the insulation efficiency at a maximum throughout the trip. The vapor barrier liner also prevents heavy ice build up and allows the bags to be easily stuffed for transport—a frozen bag has to be carried stiff and straight.

Vapor barriers do not have to be uncomfortable. By using a coated nylon, with the softer nylon side against your body, and by wearing polypropylene, or better, Polartec™

underwear, the coldness of a plastic coating and the clamminess of moisture build up from insensible perspiration loss can be avoided. A balaclava hat and scarf minimizes head exposure to cold air and cuts down on the dreaded bellows effect.

"Twining two sleeping bags and sharing them with another mammal, such as a human or dog, will extend the comfort range of your sleeping system another 25 degrees or so.

"I've used this system in sub-zero weather for weeks at a time and have never been cold or uncomfortable."

Dr. Bill Forgey

PICKING A PACK

There are external and internal frame packs, duluth sacks and packbaskets, wanigans, dry bags, duffels and a host of hard-to-classify designs. What's best for you depends on what you can afford and how seriously you pursue your dream.

Choose a soft pack for mountain climbing, canoeing (pack frames are an abomination in a canoe!), day hiking and cross country skiing. Otherwise, opt for the old aluminum frame pack. What doesn't fit inside a frame pack is easily tied to a horizontal brace. A nylon back strap or mesh panel encourages ventilation and prevents hard items from gouging your back.

For greatest comfort, pack light objects on the bottom of the pack, heavier ones on top. Reversing the procedure reduces comfort (the load tends to pull away from your body) but increases balance and control, especially on steep switch-back trails.

Many modern backpackers scorn frame packs, insisting they are too fragile and unwieldy for off-trail hiking. But some very experienced hikers disagree, as the following testimony reveals.

In Defense of External Frame Packs

by Bill Simpson

Bill Simpson teaches children with special needs and coaches the cross-country ski team in Stillwater, Minnesota. For the past 20 years he has led groups of students on wilderness adventures and for 12 years has been the leader for the American Lung Association of Minnesota wilderness trekking program, planning and leading numerous backpacking, skiing and canoeing trips all over the northern part of the continent (CJ).

"Both internal and external frame backpacks work well. Choosing one or the other is a personal choice, one which may be affected by how much you can afford to spend. Good external frame packs cost considerably less than comparable packs with internal stays. The trend over the past few years has been towards internal frames, while the "old-fashioned" externals have been largely overlooked, which may explain the price discrepancy.

The big advantage of internal frames comes when transporting them to and from the wilderness. They stack better in planes and cars; there is no frame to "grab" or break, and they "nest" easily in corners and small spaces. But a good external frame pack is as comfortable, loads well, adjusts well to your body and is easier to take on or off and put on the ground in an upright position. There is also more room on the outside to strap on sleeping bags, tents, ice axes, etc., thus gaining space on an extended expedition.

An external frame pack does "sway" a bit more when you walk, but this only becomes a concern when you're doing technical climbing or careening downhill on skis. External frame packs will not disappear from the scene, but choices are limited compared to the more popular packs with internal frames. A recent catalog from a large outdoor mail order firm has one page showing three models of external frame packs versus four pages of internal frames. My favorite? The old Kelty Tioga. I've had mine for 17 years and have yet to find a newer model I would prefer."

Tip: *tape down the straps or better, place the pack inside a strong plastic or fabric sack before transporting it in the baggage compartment of a train or airplane.*

PACK FABRICS AND FITTINGS

Nearly all packs these days are constructed from polyurethane coated (waterproof) nylon which, by all accounts, appears to be ideal for the purpose. So why is it that the Kelty Company—which traditionally used porous nylon for all their packs—refused to adopt coated material until decreased sales in the 1970's forced them to do so? Kelty also held fast to nickel-plated brass zippers long after everyone else in the industry had switched to plastic. In a similar vein, continued demand for natural canvas packs has kept Duluth Tent and Awning Company busy for more than 100 years.

The answer is simple: the camping industry is driven by consumer demand which, regrettably, is more in tune with style than function. Better that products should "look good" at the All Stars game than perform effectively outdoors. For example, most shell parkas have such narrow ("tailored") sleeves that your arms will bind if you wear anything bulky under them. I cherish my old Kelty wind-shell with its balloon sleeves and drawstring hem. Its clown-like design draws smirks in town and looks of envy afield. Like their porous nylon packs, Kelty discontinued these wonderful parkas long ago.

Consider two identical hiking packs—one built from polyurethane coated nylon, the other constructed from porous material. Both packs have seams and zippers which will readily admit water, plus closing flaps that do not have watertight seals. Submerge both packs during a stream crossing and their contents will be equally wet. In rain, the "waterproof" pack has the edge, at least for a few hours until the water soaks through the vulnerable openings.

Of course, you can glue up seams to weatherproof them, but this won't keep pack contents dry during a stream crossing or canoe capsize. Seam-sealant alone cannot close the many openings in the typical hiking pack. For this reason, experienced hikers place important items in plastic bags before they pack them.

This three step "sandwich" method ensures you'll always have dry gear no matter how hard it rains:

1. Place items in a fabric bag which need not be waterproof.

2. Close this bag and nest it inside a slightly larger waterproof plastic bag. Hug the bag to exhaust the air; twist, fold over, and seal the neck of the bag with a rubber band.

3. Set this unit inside an oversize nylon bag which need not be watertight.

Note that the tear-prone plastic liner is protected on each side by abrasion-proof nylon!

Pack everything you want to keep dry by this "sandwich" method.

Scenario: two hikers, who have packed their gear by the sandwich method, encounter a fierce rain. The man's pack is constructed from waterproof nylon; the woman's is built from porous material. By noon, the storm subsides and the sun comes out. Its penetrating heat dries the pack fabric and wet surface of the plastic bags which are inside the woman's pack (the water evaporates through the porous walls of the pack). But the inside walls of the man's pack stay drenched because rain that got in through zipper openings and seams cannot evaporate through the polyurethane coated pack fabric. The solution is to dump the pack contents and expose the inside walls of the pack to the blazing sun—a frustrating process.

Unless the hiker performs this ritualistic "dump and dry" procedure after every rain—or covers his/her "waterproof" pack with a rain poncho—moisture will cling to the inside pack fabric and encourage the growth of microorganisms. Eventually, obnoxious odors will result as the polyurethane coating of the pack is consumed by microbes.

As you can see, drying out after a rain is much easier if you use the "sandwich" method inside a pack built from porous material. "Old fashioned" canvas packs remain popular among experienced bush travelers because they are breathable, watertight and (unlike nylon) don't deteriorate in the sun. However, wet canvas is heavy and it dries slowly, the reason why backpackers don't like it. But for canoeing, horse packing and Jeep camping, where weight is less critical, canvas packs are excellent.[5]

Pack straps and fittings: Leather straps and solid brass buckles, as every modern hiker will attest, are passe. Nylon webbing, plastic fasteners and foam-filled nylon shoulder straps are lighter, easier to adjust, more durable and comfortable than those built from hide or metal.

There's no denying that synthetic fittings are lighter and more adjustable than those built from traditional materials. But they are not as durable. Quick: what's the first thing to fail on a packsack? If you answered "shoulder straps", you're absolutely correct. First to go is the nylon material which encases the foam-filled straps. Next, are the grommets and stitching which secure the straps. In time, the cushy foam which feels so comfortable when new, compacts and dies.

Replacing straps on a Kelty style external frame outfit is straightforward and simple: pull two spring clips, pop the

[5]Duluth Tent, Inc., Box 16024, Duluth, MN 55816-0024; phone: 218-722-3898, offers a variety of packs, luggage and accessories built from leather-trimmed canvas. The company will custom make packs, tarps and tents to your specifications. Their catalog is free.

pins and the unit is free—five minutes work, if you have the parts on hand. The same job on a high-tech internal frame outfit may require disassembly of the pack yoke, plus major re-sewing.

On the other hand, if a leather strap breaks (usually at a buckle) in the field, just cut off the damaged part and sew or rivet the remains back together. If stitching pulls loose at the yoke, a needle and thread will easily fix it. Leather, as everyone knows, is infinitely tougher than nylon. Indeed, leather straps and metal fittings invariably outlive the packs to which they were originally attached.

As to comfort, the jury is out. Many hikers (myself included) still prefer supple leather shoulder straps to sloshy foam-filled nylon ones. Compare a synthetic bike or horse saddle to a form-fitted top grain leather one and you'll see why. Plastics and foam cost much less than oil-tanned leather and nickel-plated brass—reason enough for their popularity. Fact is, a modern pack built from top grade canvas with leather and brass fittings would cost a fortune. It would also be heavier and more durable than one made from nylon and plastic.

Hip belt: Every serious backpacker relies on a hip belt to take the sting out of a heavy load. Snug the thickly padded belt around your waist, slightly loosen the shoulder straps, and feel the weight transfer from your shoulders to your lower body. When your hips get tired, just release the belt and keep on walking.

Tumpline: attach a wide leather or canvas strap to a pack, and you have a tumpline. Place the strap just above your forehead, lean forward into the trace, and shuffle confidently down the trail. The early canoe men carried 180 pounds and more across rugged portages using only this rig, and packers in undeveloped countries still rely on it for toting heavy loads.

The beauty of the tumpline is threefold: 1) it can be quickly removed from one load and attached to another; 2) the weight is supported by your head and neck muscles which, as every Himalayan Sherpa will attest, are stronger

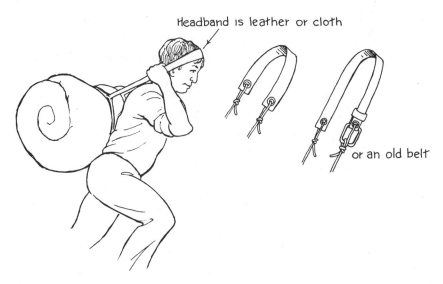

Headband is leather or cloth

or an old belt

Figure 6-5

than those in your shoulders; 3) the load is held tightly against your back, even when ascending steep hills. Carry a heavy load up a steep incline on packstraps alone and feel the weight pull you backwards. Now, add a tumpline. Immediately, the load shifts forward, the swaying stops, and you regain control. The effect is so pronounced that you'll want a tumpline on all your packs.

Wilderness canoeists know all about tumplines, though backpackers have not yet learned to spell the word. And that's unfortunate, because what works on a canoe pack works on a hiking pack.

Note: best way to use a tumpline is to transfer the pack weight from one suspension system to another, as needed. For example, when your shoulders get tired, change to the hip belt, then to the tumpline or shoulder straps. A snug hip belt and shoulder straps (no tumpline) provides the best control on down hill descents, while a firm tumpstrap and light shoulder straps are better when ascending a grade. Allow your body to experiment and you'll discover that variety is the essence of comfort!

RAINGEAR

Scenario: the temperature drops logarithmically as clouds of twisted black mass threateningly overhead. When the mercury reaches 40, the sky lets loose with a torrent of rain, whipped by winds of 30 miles an hour. High on a treeless ridge, you continue the hike, for inside your expensive storm suit, you are warm and dry. You smile at your friend nearby who is clad in an outfit which costs half the price of yours. Slyly, he returns the grin and announces that he is also warm and dry. C'mon now; equal performance at half the price? What gives?

Welcome to the club! Here's one place where high cost and reliability don't always go hand-in-hand. Protected pockets, under-arm zippers, double-drawstring hoods that turn with your head, color-coded ventilation panels and tailored sleeves cost money. Big money! Forgo complex tailoring and non-essential bells and whistles, and you'll get by for less. The mystery is solved: your friend is no fool!

My advice? For severe weather, choose the same rain gear that professional foresters and construction workers wear. Some discount store rain outfits are very reliable, as are many mid-priced equipment store suits. Expect to pay obscene prices for breathable/waterproof materials.

What you wear under your rain gear is important. Begin with a wicking layer of polypropylene, wool or polyester long underwear next to the skin, then put on a wool, pile or acrylic shirt. Save your rain coat for rain and wear a porous shell parka for protection from wind as you hike or work around camp. If you wear rain gear for casual wind protection, as advised by some "experts", it will soon develop holes and tears that will admit water when it rains.

TOYS

A butane lighter, flashlight, Sierra cup for a ladle, Leatherman™, duct tape, parachute cord and small sewing kit will suffice for the short trip. Extended stays require a full battery of supportive toys—everything from instant epoxy to replacement gaskets for the stove.

It's impossible to describe all you need to have—and need to know—in a chapter of this length. So don't neglect your studies. Join a hiking, climbing or canoeing club; attend outdoor seminars, and read every book on camping you can get your hands on before you take to the backcountry. After all, it's one thing to own good gear; it's another to know how to use it effectively!

CHAPTER

seven

• • •

Camp Gadgets
and Accessories

I grew up in Chicago in the 1940's, but never took the "city part" too seriously. Back of our three story apartment building were acres of rugged hills (an abandoned housing project) which butted a then unpolluted stream. We named the place "bicycle paradise" for the trails which challenged our single speed Schwinns. When summer vacation finally came, we packed a Spartan kit and made for the hills. Once, we camped by the creek a full week, with only a blanket, tin can cook-set and pocket knife. First night it rained and never let up the whole week. None of us had rain coats or waterproof shoes: we just rigged two ponchos and fed small twigs into a smoky tin stove we made from an old water bucket. Though we struggled constantly with the fire, I don't remember being cold or wet. The excitement of youth, I suppose.

On my 12th birthday, dad took me to Abercrombie and Fitch which, in the 1950's, was Chicago's premier outdoor store. There were racks of expensive shotguns and rifles, cases of fine knives, packsacks, tents and camping accessories—everything one needed for camping out. It was all so wonderful . . . and so expensive. For months, I'd pestered Dad about getting me a folding Sterno stove to simplify cooking at bicycle paradise. Maybe, just maybe, he would buy one for me today!

Then, I saw it—its gleaming brass tank and galvanized metal case gave it away. Rutstrum, Steffanson, Byrd and the other great explorers had said this was the one to get. With a trembling voice I asked the salesman if I could see the "Primus 71".

Scarcely larger than a pint carton of milk, the little stove weighed just 18 ounces. It had no pump: you used the heat of your hands or an eyedropper filled with gas to prime it. The price tag read five dollars, which I knew was out of the question.

Slowly, I pushed the Primus away. "Got any Sterno stoves?" I asked weakly. Then, a miracle. "We'll take it," said dad, as he reached for his wallet. Talk about making a kid happy! Forty years, a needle valve and two wicks later, the Primus continues to run. Though I have newer stoves which are lighter, more powerful and less temperamental than the old Primus, I continue to use it on solo trips simply because it brings me joy.

For the same reason, I sometimes make wood or metal camp gadgets that I could buy in stores. Why spend minutes whittling pot hooks when you can buy stainless steel chain and S-hooks in every hardware store? Or, cook soup in a number ten can when genuine pots can be bought for next to nothing? Does it make sense to handicap yourself with an "oil can" cook stove, wooden fork and spoon, tin can cup, Ozark pan oven or packsack made from discarded blue jeans when you can buy the real thing at a price you can afford?

Absolutely, if it brings you joy! There's smug satisfaction in self-reliance, in coping expertly with what's on hand. To this end, I offer this chapter, the contents of which were once "serious stuff" in turn-of-the-century books which are long out-of-print. Just for fun, light your camp with a tin can lantern you've made yourself, sip soup from a spoon you've carved with your pocket knife; fry fish in an old steel pan on a galvanized bucket stove like the one I used as a kid.

Then, laze back and grin heartily. Congratulations, friend. You've discovered the joy of camping out!

TIN CAN ART

Tin Bucket Stove   Cut openings in a galvanized tin bucket as shown in figure 7-1. Holes punched in the back work as well as the rectangular chimney that's illustrated. If you're energetic, you can make a circular hole in the back then fit a stove pipe made from tin cans. In the old days we'd friction fit the cans together and accept what smoke leaked through the joints. Now, there's duct tape.

Hobo Stove   You'll need a three pound coffee can or gallon paint can. A lid is essential to extinguish the stove and to seal the ashes inside when you pack up.

Punch quarter inch diameter holes around the base of the open can, 1-2 inches from the bottom. Make the holes larger if you want more draft, smaller (as when using charcoal) for less draft. Punch another ring of holes just beneath the top, so the flame won't go out when you set a pan on the burner.

Put a half inch layer of sand or gravel on the bottom (optional) so the stove won't burn out, and place charcoal or wood on top of this. You can speed ignition with kerosine or charcoal lighter, if you prefer, though the stove will start fine without it.

The Zip stove, a very efficient commercial version of the Hobo stove, is available from ZZ Corporation, 10806 Kaylor St., Los Alamitos, CA 90720. Powered by a tiny electric motor and AA battery, the little Zip stove starts instantly and burns with a pulsating red-blue flame that develops about 14,000 BTU's, or nearly twice the heat of most liquid fuel stoves. The tiny stove weighs barely a pound, complete with engine and sliding damper. Optional accessories include a grill and windscreen. The unit is quite inexpensive.

Bucket Stove

Figure 7-1

I've used the Zip stove quite a bit on my canoe trips in the barren lands, where wood is a prize commodity. It burns pencil-thin twigs, pine cones, charcoal and muskox "chips" with a vengeance. Its one drawback is a voracious appetite for fuel.

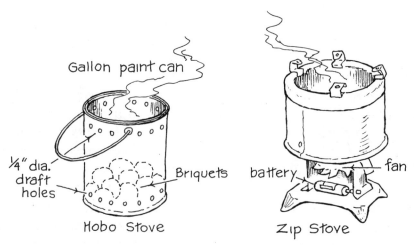

Figure 7-2

Sand or dirt
saturated
with 50/50
motor oil-
gas mix

G-I C-Ration Stove

Figure 7-3

GI C-Ration Stove   I heated many cans of C-rations on this stove when I was an artillery forward observer in Germany in the 1960's. Same principle as the Hobo stove but without holes at the bottom. Fill the can half full of sand or dirt and pour in a half pint of kerosine, alcohol, or motor oil cut 50 percent with gasoline.

Safety concerns: the liquid fuel won't extinguish with water so keep a tin lid and pail of sand handy. Be sure the stove is well supported: if it tips, burning fuel will spill all over the country side. The hazards of this unit suggest that the stove never be used indoors, by children or irresponsible adults. Obnoxious fuel odors (except when burning alcohol) will get into any meats you roast, so limit stove use to food in pots.

Hobo Oven   A large square can works best, but a round one will do. Punch a row of holes around the can, about one-third the way up from the bottom, as illustrated in figure 7-4, and make a grill from lengths of bailing wire or peeled, green sticks. Place your bakestuff on the supports, close the "door", and set the oven on a low fire or your trail stove. Baking time is about the same as your home oven.

Tip: *if you line the bottom of the oven with sand or stones, it will heat more evenly and be less likely to warp from the heat.*

Figure 7-4

Tin Can, Foil Oven   Line the bottom of a three pound coffee can with stones and place an aluminum foil tray on top of the stones. Put your bakestuff in the tray, cover the can with an aluminum plate or foil, and set the "oven" on a low fire or your trail stove.

To use this hobo appliance as a steamer to cook vegetables and rehydrate fruit, pour water into the can just below the level of the stones. Set fruit or veggies on the stones or on a crude stick rack above the stones. Add a lightly vented cover and apply heat. Essentially, you've created a tin "bamboo steamer". To "steam bake", place bread dough in an open plastic bag and set the bag on the steamer rack. Cover the oven and relax for 20 minutes.

Gasoline or Vegetable Oil Can, Reflector Oven   Cut and bend the can as illustrated in figure 7-5, and set the oven before a hot fire. Reflector ovens work best when highly polished, so keep fine steel wool and Bon Ami handy.

Three in One Stove   With this clever rig you can bake, fry and boil all at one time. A standard, triangular can puncher is used to make the smoke holes. You'll need two

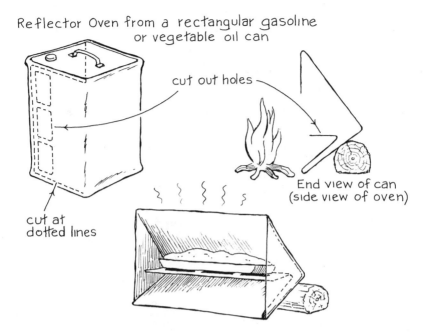

Reflector Oven from a rectangular gasoline
or vegetable oil can

cut out holes

End view of can
(side view of oven)

cut at
dotted lines

Figure 7-5

3-pound coffee cans to make the stove, plus a pair of smaller cans for the oven and broiler. Manufacture and assembly requires only a few minutes. Figure 7-6 shows the procedure.

Hobo Walking Lantern Remove one end of a large tin can, punch two holes along a side and install a wire (not string!) carrying handle, as illustrated in figure 7-7. Punch more holes nearby to provide ventilation for the candle. Keep holes away from the handle area or you may burn your hands when you carry the lantern.

Set a short, fat candle inside the can, closer to the back than the front. You can "glue" down the candle with melted wax or impale it on a short nail punched through the bottom of the can. Caution: don't use this lantern inside a tent!

Tin Can Water Faucet When I was a kid in the 1950's, I spent several summers at a rustic scout camp deep in the Michigan woods. There were no cabins in those days, just

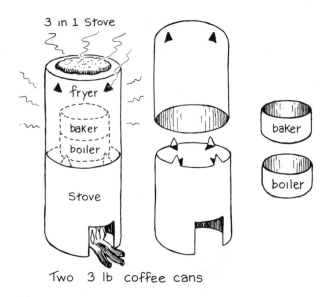

Figure 7-6

big wall tents with wooden floors. One hundred yards away was an outhouse and long handled pump. In place of showers, we swam in the lake.

The rules called for washing up before meals, and older kids were assigned the task of checking hands and faces. Since the water pump was located so far away, we relied on a tin can wash stand like the one illustrated in figure 7-8.

A large tin can, wooden stick plug and some string are all you need to make the apparatus. Water flow is controlled by varying the fit of the plug in the hole. Wash water can be

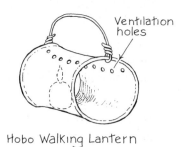

Hobo Walking Lantern

Figure 7-7

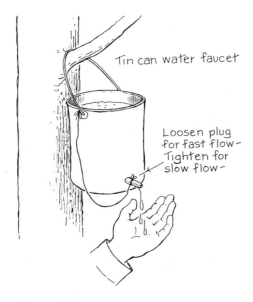

Figure 7-8

trapped in a bucket below and reused. Heat the can (rotate the plug away from flames so it doesn't burn) on a stove or fire if you want hot water.

Tin Can Pasta Drainer and Stove Case   When I was in the army, one of the men had a small liquid fuel stove, similar to the now famous PEAK 1. To protect the stove in transit, he stored it in a large tin can which had a wire bail handle and holes punched in the bottom. When I questioned him about the holes, he replied that the can was his "pasta strainer".

Figure 7-9 shows some other zany tin can projects.

HANDY "AP" PAPER DISPENSER

Toilet paper—or "all purpose" paper as the scouts call it—is a multifunctional essential that earns its pay as a facial and first aid tissue, dish towel, absorbent sponge and tool cleaner. Dry "AP" paper is a precious commodity in

Tin can Projects

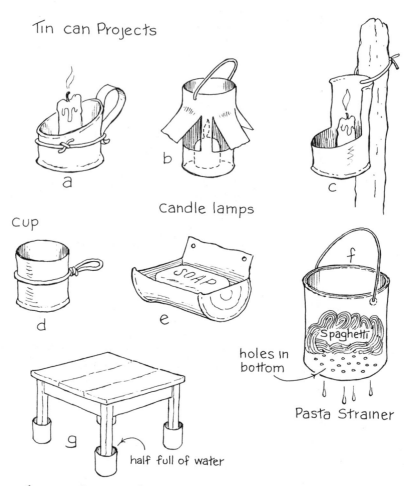

Candle lamps

cup

holes in bottom

Spaghetti

Pasta Strainer

half full of water

To keep "crawlers" from food table

Figure 7-9

the backcountry. Rick Garza, a Texas scoutleader suggests this ingenious method of keeping it that way:

Firmly crush the roll and pull out the cardboard tube. Grab the end of the roll at the center of the core and pull it out through the core. Sheets should stream continuously from the center of the core like they do from a Kleenex™ box.

Now, place the flattened "AP" roll inside a tight-fitting Ziplock™ bag. The plastic bag protects the bulk roll from rain as you pull needed paper through the slit-like mouth of the bag. Use this same procedure to dispense paper toweling. Hint: saw the paper towel roll in half first so that the size is more manageable.

JACK-KNIFE CAMPFIRE AIDS

Figure 7-10 shows a number of campfire aids that you can whittle with your pocket-knife. Some, like the "swinging fire crane" and "split wood fork" are so useful that you'll want them whenever you cook on an open fire. Others, like the "fire tongs" and "hot pan holder" are more therapeutic than practical.

"Jack-Knife Campfire Aids"

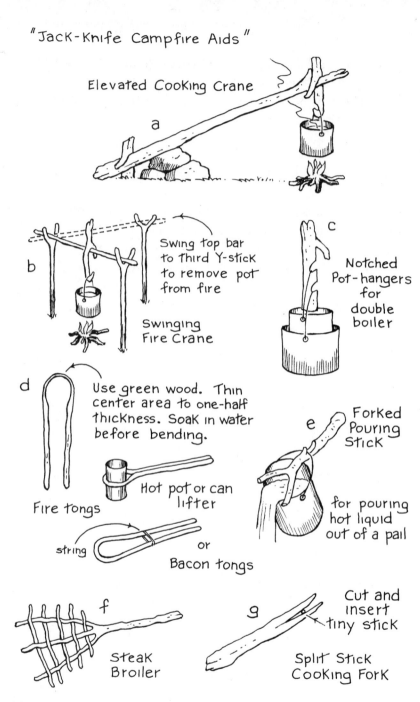

Elevated Cooking Crane

a

b Swing top bar to third Y-stick to remove pot from fire

Swinging Fire Crane

c Notched Pot-hangers for double boiler

d Use green wood. Thin center area to one-half thickness. Soak in water before bending.

Fire tongs

Hot pot or can lifter

string or Bacon tongs

e Forked Pouring Stick

for pouring hot liquid out of a pail

f Steak Broiler

g Cut and insert tiny stick

Split Stick Cooking Fork

Figure 7-10

CHAPTER

eight

• • •

Pack Tricks

I grew up in the slide rule era of the 1950's when "three place accuracy" was the norm. At that, it was necessary to interpolate digits carefully and mentally figure the decimal point to get a reasonable answer.

Now, there's the speedy calculator which eliminates all errors. Decimals are accurately placed, instantly! There's no need for mental gymnastics. Or thought. Simply push some buttons and the numbers pop into view. No need to know multiplication tables, decimal rules or percent formulas to do math problems.

Don't you believe it! Math and science teachers will tell you that many young people (and adults too) rely so heavily on calculators that they cannot perform basic math functions without them. And God forbid their quick fingers should misplace a number or decimal point on the keyboard. If the lighted display shows 45.60, when simple logic suggests it should read 4.56, so be it. The machine is always right.

Ditto when it comes to how to pack a pack. In the days when "soft packs" reigned supreme, every hiker knew the ropes. Scout manuals and outdoor books of the day be-labored item placement, weight distribution and efficient utilization of space. Now, there is no need for such information because we have modern packs with comfort-contoured frames which, like calculators, (supposedly) compensate for user errors. Experienced hikers know better. Like them, you'll discover that no matter what kind of pack you own, there's comfort in "doing it right."

BALANCE AND CONVENIENCE

The Wilderness Education Association—an organization whose mission is to professionalize outdoor leadership, improve the safety of outdoor trips and conserve wild places[1]—has coined the term "conveniently balanced system" (CBS) to teach proper packing methods. The acronym reminds novices that "where you put what," is influenced by "what you need when."

WEA instructors Jack Drury, Bruce Bonney and David Cockrell, espouse the CBS principle in the organization's bible, *The Wilderness Educator* (ICS Books, 1991):

> "The itinerary for the day should be considered when packing a pack, and the arrangement of equipment in the pack should reflect the probability of equipment use during the day. External pockets should hold items that are predicted to be most frequently needed ...Items (like first aid and repair kits) that may be needed quickly for safety or other reasons should be packed in known areas of easy access.
>
> Heavy loads are most comfortably carried when the weight is placed directly in line with the largest and strongest bones and muscles of the body: the pelvic girdle, the upper thigh bones, and the muscles of the thighs and buttocks. Thus, the heaviest part of the pack should usually be centered as close to the body and as near to the top of the spinal column as possible. Heavy loads are most comfortable when they're balanced left to right, top to bottom, and front to back.

[1]Wilderness Education Association, 20 Winona Ave., Box 89, Saranac Lake, NY 12983, Phone: (518) 891-2915 ext. 254

The terrain over which the hiker will pass should also influence the way weight is distributed. For flat, easily traveled terrain, the pack may be packed for maximum comfort with the center of gravity near the shoulders and close to the body. For rough terrain, steep inclines, talus hopping, river crossing, etc.—the center of gravity should be lower to improve balance.

A pack that is organized according to an efficient and consistently maintained system speeds daily packing and makes it easier to find things. Individual items of equipment should be grouped together and packed in stuff sacks. For example, one might have a toilet kit, clothes bag, food bag, personal repair kit, 'night' bag, etc. Packers should strive to keep their packs streamlined and neat. All items of equipment should be placed inside the pack bag and its contents securely lashed to the pack frame to avoid annoying losses on the trail. No odds and ends should be tied on or protrude from the pack sack. Tent poles, ice axes or other long items should be lashed along the vertical line of the pack to prevent their becoming impediments to progress through narrow passages."

EVERY CUBIC INCH COUNTS!

To fit a three-season sleeping bag, foam pad, change of clothes, rain gear, cook-set, stove and ten days rations into the typical hiking pack calls for careful planning, even if you know what you're doing. These tricks will help you smooth the way.

The best hiking packs are patterned to follow the curvature of the human spine. To maintain this curve (which is an expensive, high tech feature), you must pack your gear in horizontal rather than vertical layers, with each layer running from side-wall to side-wall as illustrated in figure 8-1.

To accomplish this, stuff sacks are best matched to the dimensions of the pack; that is, they should be long enough to fit crossways with no wasted space at the ends. To

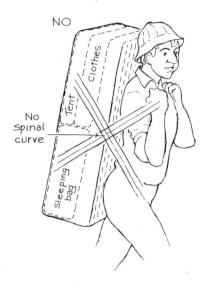

Figure 8-1

reduce packed volume, some hikers place bulky items like sleeping bags and clothes in special "compression sacks" which have straps that squeeze the load at the ends. Compression bags do save space, but they foul up the whole packing system unless they are designed to fit the pack. I know of only one manufacturer (GRADE VI, LTD., Urbana, IL 61801-0008) who offers tailored compression sacks which are designed to fit specific pack models. GRADE VI sacks fill and compress from the sides rather than the ends—an ingenious feature which utilizes every cubic inch of pack space.

You can use the GRADE VI space-filling principle to construct stuff sacks which precisely fit your hiking pack. Simply make the sacks long and narrow rather than short and fat (the industry standard).

Tip: no need to use polyurethane-coated nylon to make your stuff sacks. Porous fabric is lighter and easier to wash than water-proof stuff, and it doesn't retain odors. If you pack your gear by the "sandwich" method suggested in chapter 6, you'll never have to eat damp oatmeal.

Here's a fast, efficient way to pack your pack:

First, line the packsack with a strong, waterproof plastic bag. The bag should be one and one-half times the length of the pack.

Next, place a fabric "abrasion liner" inside the waterproof plastic bag. The abrasion liner can be sewn from porous nylon, polypropylene or Dacron™. It does not have to be waterproof. Pack items in this order:

1. Set the "sandwich-packed" sleeping bag crossways on the bottom of the pack. If you've used a properly sized stuff sack, the sleeping bag will reach from wall to wall.

2. Your foam sleeping pad goes next, followed by another fitted stuff sack filled with spare clothes. Rafters and canoeists will want to waterproof their clothes by the "sandwich" method: hikers can dispense with this precaution.

3. Next comes food and stove, each appropriately bagged in color-coded nylon.

4. Now, hug the bag to exhaust air and pleat and roll the abrasion liner. The tent, sans poles and stakes goes next, fitting inside the waterproof bag like a cork in a bottle.

5. Tightly roll down the waterproof plastic bag; place your rain gear, sweater, wind garments and rain tarp on top, and cinch down the pack flap. Tent poles and stakes are packed in a special bag which is either lashed vertically to the frame or side-wall D-rings of a hiking pack, or set under the pack-flap of a "Duluth style" canoe pack.

Tip: *to keep tent poles from sliding out beneath a loose pack flap, sew a loop of parachute cord to each end of the pole bag and snake the closing straps of the pack flap through the cord loops.*

6. First-aid and repair kit, sun-glasses, map and compass, snacks and other frequently needed items go in the zippered side pockets of the pack.

Note that the sealed abrasion liner separates the tent (which may be wet and muddy) from the dry pack contents below. The heaviest items—tent, food and cooking gear—reside near the top of the pack, which is usually the most comfortable arrangement. And everything is conveniently located as the following scenario illustrates:

It begins to rain heavily just as you reach camp. First order of business is to erect overhead shelter so you can un-pack and prepare meals in comfort. Un-clip the pack flap—the rain tarp is right on top. Soon as the tarp is rigged, you can go about pitching the tent, which is the next item in your packsack. Note that the strong abrasion liner remains sealed when the tent is removed from the pack—a protective feature which prevents stray raindrops from falling on food, clothing and sleeping gear below.

Now that the tent is pitched you can turn your attention to establishing the kitchen and preparing your sleeping system. Everything you need is at hand, out of the weather, and conveniently located in the order you'll need it. What could be simpler?

IMPROVISED PACKS

Say you're out for a walk and come upon an armful of dry kindling and need a container to carry it home. The illustrations below show several old-fashioned ways to rig a hasty pack.

Pack Harness and Tumpline Pack   When I was a kid, I relied on a small canvas pup tent, rubberized poncho and GI issue wool blanket sleeping bag for all my camping. Though these items were acceptably light for backpacking, they were much too bulky to fit into the confines of my pre-war haversack. Larger packs were available, of course, but I had no money for them. So I simply rolled everything into a single waterproof bundle and rigged a pack harness or tumpline.

Procedure: Set your poncho or nylon trail tarp flat on the ground and place your unrolled tent on top. Put your plastic ground cloth on top of the tent and lay unrolled sleeping bags and foam pads or air mattresses over this. Fold in the sides and ends of the plastic ground cloth to make a waterproof envelope.

Next, fold in the sides and ends of the tent and tarp and roll up everything. Secure the roll with straps or cord and rig a pack harness (figure 8-2) and/or tumpline (figure 6-5). This packing method disposes of all your bulky items (saves stuffing them into tight-fitting sacks each morning) in one unit.

Hobo Pack   Place a large, smooth pebble into each corner of a grain or pillow sack. Twist the pebbles and tie ropes around them (like a ball and garter device) to form crude shoulder straps, as illustrated in figure 8-3. Pad your shoulders with a shirt or jacket.

Cub Scout Pants Pack   When I was an eight year old cub scout, there was a kid in my pack who carried his gear in a pair of worn out blue jeans. The pant legs were tied off as shoulder straps and items were lashed inside the waist, as illustrated in figure 8-4. Primitive though it looked, the little pants pack was surprisingly comfortable with small, light loads.

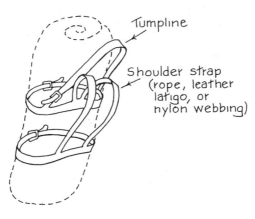

Figure 8-2

Hobo Pack (grain sack or pillow case)

pad shoulders with shirt or jacket

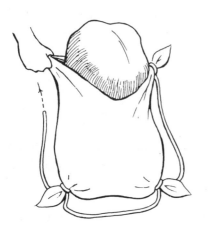

Figure 8-3

Cub Scout Pants Pack

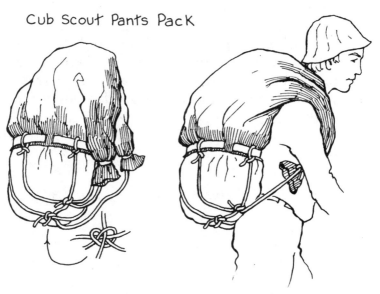

Figure 8-4

CHAPTER
nine
● ● ●

Backwoods
Communication

It happened in 1962, a few days before final exams at Purdue University. Friends and I were cramming for a test while listening to light classical music on our short wave receiver. Evidently, the weather conditions were just right, for the Moscow ballet came in loud and clear.

Suddenly, the broadcast was interrupted by the mechanical trill of Morse code. Dit, dit, dit, dah, dah, dah, dit, dit dit, it hammered, again and again. The S-O-S was obvious, but not the letters which followed.

I had walked the Scouting trail from tenderfoot to eagle, learning Morse code as part of the first class requirement. Communications and ships had always fascinated me, so when I was in high school I joined a "sea explorer" post and practiced with blinker and semaphore. I could send and receive Morse code at about three words a minute—a fraction the speed of commercial transmissions.

Following the S-O-S came the ship's name and position (latitude and longitude). All this was repeated, again and again. It took me half an hour to translate what a pro could do in minutes. I plotted the location on a small globe: it was about 200 miles off the coast of Australia. By now,

45 minutes had passed and the ship was still signalling for help. I wondered why no one else had heeded the call.

Friends urged me to contact the Coast Guard immediately. But I was unsure of my skills and certain that rescue units were already on the way. Besides, the "skip" transmission was coming from Russia, thousands of miles away. It seemed preposterous that others had not heard the call. I dismissed the idea, went back to the books . . . and another radio station.

We closed the study session at two a.m. and switched back to radio Moscow to see if the ship was still sending code. It was. Then, we went to bed, certain that help was forthcoming.

When I returned from class the next day I was greeted by the somber face of my friend. Seems as if I had indeed correctly deciphered the S-O-S. The freighter went down just where I had plotted it. The news said that distress signals were received at three a.m. that morning, four hours after I had turned a deaf ear. I sat down and cried, and 30 years later, still wonder why I acted so stupidly.

With today's satellites and compact short-wave radios, you can make a very good case for not learning Morse code. Nonetheless, a knowledge of code can be surprisingly useful. For example, suppose you're verbally transmitting a distress signal deep in the wilderness, and like the ship, no one hears your call. As batteries grow dimmer with use, the message becomes more and more garbled. When your plea for help is finally received, your words are unintelligible.

Fortunately, the crisp "dit, dah's" of Morse code can save the day. You can use a whistle, bugle, crow or moose call, or you can make a rasping sound on a tin pot or piece of wood. Even a verbal "dit-dah" can be used in place of words. Like men who have been trapped in mine shafts and submarines, you can tap out the dots and dashes on an aluminum kettle, using fast, light taps on the edge for dots (shorts) and heavy, slow taps in the center for dashes (longs).

INTERNATIONAL
MORSE CODE: Figure 9-1

A	dot-dash	
B	dash-dot-dot-dot	
C	dash-dot-dash-dot	
D	dash-dot-dot	
E	dot	
F	dot-dot-dash-dot	
G	dash-dash-dot	
H	dot-dot-dot-dot	
I	dot-dot	
J	dot-dash-dash-dash	
K	dash-dot-dash	
L	dot-dash-dot-dot	
M	dash-dash	
N	dash-dot	
O	dash-dash-dash	
P	dot-dash-dash-dot	
Q	dash-dash-dot-dash	
R	dot-dash-dot	
S	dot-dot-dot	
T	dash	
U	dot-dot-dash	
V	dot-dot-dot-dash	
W	dot-dash-dash	
X	dash-dot-dot-dash	
Y	dash-dot-dash-dash	
Z	dash-dash-dot-dot	

NUMERALS

1. dot-dash-dash-dash-dash
2. dot-dot-dash-dash-dash
3. dot-dot-dot-dash-dash
4. dot-dot-dot-dot-dash
5. dot-dot-dot-dot-dot
6. dash-dot-dot-dot-dot
7. dash-dash-dot-dot-dot
8. dash-dash-dash-dot-dot
9. dash-dash-dash-dash-dot
10. dash-dash-dash-dash-dash

Figure 9-1

If you can't create a difference in sound by tapping on a bucket in different ways, use the telegrapher's quick tap-tap for a "short", and tap (interval of silence) tap, for a "long". For example, the letter L (dot, dash, dot, dot) would be drummed out as tap-tap . . . tap (silence) tap . . . tap-tap . . . tap-tap.

You can also "wigwag" Morse code with a flag, branch, hat or canoe paddle, as illustrated in figure 9-2. A series of right-to-left overhead waves (AAAA) gets the attention of the receiver, who responds with a "K" (dash, dot, dash) when he or she is ready to view your message.

Make a dot by waving the flag to the right, a dash by waving left. Dip the flag forward and down to pause between words and sentences. Pause after each word to allow the receiver to wigwag an acknowledging "K" (dash, dot, dash). If you receive "IMI" (do not understand) instead of the affirmative "K", repeat the word and pause again. If you make an error or want to cancel the word, dip the flag and signal eight dots (E's), then dip and re-start the word. "AR" indicates that the message is complete. "R" acknowledges receipt.

At night, messages can be transmitted by flashlight or campfire blinker signals. A blanket or coat provides the darkening screen you need to block out fire light. Use the standard signals in figure 9-3 to support your message.

Morse Code by Wigwag

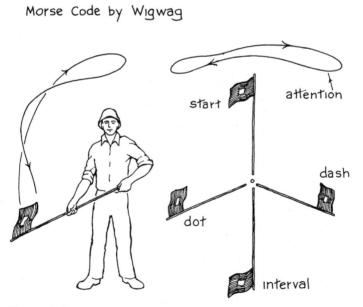

Figure 9-2

STANDARD SIGNALS

MEANING	RADIO	BLINKER LIGHT	WIGWAG
Attention, get ready to receive me:	CQ	AA	Overhead wave
I am ready to receive you:	K	K	K
Wait a moment:	AS	AS	AS
I can't receive you:	QRJ	W	Move flag: up-- down--right--left
A break, as to begin a message:	BT	BT	BT
End of sentence:	Period	AAA	AAA
End of word:	Space	Space	Flag to front
Error, will repeat:	EEEEEEE	EEEEEEE	EEEEEEE
Please repeat:	IMI	IMI	IMI
Word received	no signal	T	T
Message received:	R	R	R
End of message	AR	AR	AR

Figure 9-3

MORSE CODE BY HELIOGRAPH

It was 1967, and my first trip to the Boundary Waters Canoe Area. John Orr and I had just completed the portage into Knife Lake when we came upon two adults with a group of teenagers in tow. Amidst the canoes and equipment was a stretcher, occupied by a girl of 15.

"Whatsa matter with her?" I asked. "Stomach ache. Got some bad food," replied an adult leader.

The girl said she'd had the "stomach ache" for two days and it was getting worse. John was our high school football coach and pretty knowledgeable about medicine and injuries. "Did you give her any medications?" he asked. "Just Tums, Pepto Bismol and asprin," came the reply. John flashed me a terrified look then gently touched one side of the girl's abdomen. No reaction. He touched the other side and she screamed in pain.

Appendicitis! The girl must be evacuated immediately.

I unfolded a map and pointed to Cache Bay Ranger station on Saganaga Lake, 20 miles away. "They've got a radio there and can call for a plane." I suggested they empty a canoe and put the girl in the middle with two strong paddlers. It was barely noon and there was only one portage between Knife Lake and Saganaga. They should make the ranger station easily by supper time. Meanwhile, we'd set up some smoke signals to attract the forest service spotter (fire) plane which serviced the area.

There was opposition by the adult leaders until John made it perfectly clear that the girl would die without help. Then, a miracle: just as we were loading the girl into the canoe, we saw the Forest Service float plane overhead. Instantly, I grabbed my Silva Ranger compass and flashed its mirror across the horizon. Incredibly, the first flash caught the pilot's eye. The Cessna banked and turned our way. Nervously, I continued to flash.

As the plane approached for a better look, I ordered the kids to line up and execute the "hurry" (figure 9-4) signal by pumping their fists up and down. A wing dropped and in he came, chugging to within feet of the rocky beach.

The pilot was hopping mad. He told us we'd better have a "damn good reason" for bringing down his airplane. We pointed to the girl on the stretcher and his anger faded to concern. Carefully, we loaded her into the tiny airplane and watched it speed away. When we finished our trip a week later we learned that John's diagnosis had been correct. The girl's appendix was removed without consequences at the hospital in Grand Marais minutes after the plane set down. John's quick thinking, my mirror, and a forest service fire plane which just happened to be there, saved a life. Amazingly, it happened just that way.

In my book, *Canoeing Wild Rivers*, I tell the story of two men whose lives were saved by a flashing mirror. Though not unique, their story bears repeating here:

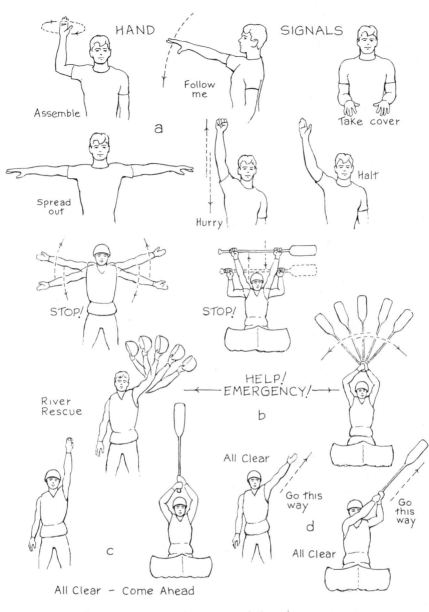

HAND SIGNALS

Assemble

Follow me

Take cover

Spread out

Hurry

Halt

STOP!

STOP!

a

River Rescue

HELP! ← EMERGENCY! →

b

All Clear

Go this way

d

Go this way

All Clear

All Clear – Come Ahead

c

Ground Rescue Signals:

X Require medical assistance

N No (or negative)

V Require assistance

Y Yes (or affirmative)

↑ Proceeding in this direction

Figure 9-4

It was 1968 and the man was a high school teacher with a free summer. His friend was a business man who had precisely 14 days vacation. The idea was to paddle about 200 miles of Manitoba's South Seal River. To save time, they'd drive to The Pas then fly commercial air to Lynn Lake. There, they would charter a float plane to the "put in". The canoe would be sent by rail from their home in Minneapolis to Lynn Lake ahead of time. Fast and neat; the canoe would be waiting for them when they arrived. Or so they thought!

First stop, Lynn Lake train station. "What, no canoe? Checking revealed that customs authorities had impounded the craft for payment of duty. No matter, the misunderstanding could be cleared up in a few days. A few days indeed! Precious time was ticking by. The business man didn't have "a few days".

So the men went shopping for a canoe. A thorough search turned up the only canoe in town—an old but relatively sound 17 foot wood-canvas Chestnut. The craft weighed at least 100 pounds, had a deep fin keel and a square stern. But it was a canoe, and it cost only 80 dollars!

Everything was going wrong. The teacher looked at the bright yellow fabric cover he had made for his Alumacraft. It wouldn't fit the Chestnut, but it might come in handy for something!

Problems compounded from the outset. Instead of averaging 25 miles per day as they had anticipated, they were making only 10. They had the wrong footwear, the wrong raingear, the wrong canoe . . . and the wrong attitude. Only the teacher's insistence that they bring a small Optimus stove saved the day. Without it they'd have been miserable in the incessant rain.

What worried them most was that they were falling drastically behind schedule. So to compensate they took to paddling well into the evening. They grew impatient and careless. On the ninth day around nine p.m., they encountered "the rapid". It looked easy enough from the top so they decided to run it blind. The moment of reckoning came quickly: man-sized rollers at the bottom swamped the canoe and the boulder field took out the keel and one gunnel.

The old Chestnut was wrecked beyond repair. The trip was over!

The men salvaged the gear and struggled to shore. An inventory of their food revealed a seven days supply. The river was too fast and narrow on which to land a float plane, so the next day they carried their outfit about six miles overland to a small lake that had a sand beach. There they devised elaborate signals—made a huge S-O-S on the beach and cut flags from their yellow canoe cover. And each afternoon the men flashed their signal mirror hopefully across the empty skies.

Twenty-one days later they were picked up by a search and rescue plane: it was the flash of light that caught the pilot's eye. Total cost of the rescue came to $3,200 dollars (a fortune in 1968), which the men paid sheepishly but gladly.

When you're hundreds of air miles from the nearest road, few things are as reliable as a mirror. There are no batteries to deplete, no electrical connections to corrode and no parts to become waterlogged or break. A small heliograph (the original military model is by far the best) is compact and rugged. In good light, a signal can be seen for 10 miles.

The emergency military signaling mirror (ESM/1) measures approximately four inches by five inches. There's a cross-shaped sighting hole in the center and a two inch diameter silvered area in back. Even with the sighting device, getting the splash of light to strike the pilot's eye is much more difficult than textbooks suggest. Here's the proven military procedure (which must be practiced!) along with ideas for making an effective heliograph in the field.

1. Hold the mirror 3–4 inches in front of your face, looking into the sun. Reflect sunlight on any nearby surface in line with the target. Tilt the mirror to shine towards the target.

2. A spot of light will come through the cross-shaped hole and fall on your face. Look for this spot in the (back) silvered portion of the mirror.

3. Move the mirror so that the spot of light on your face disappears into the cross-shaped hole. Now, maintain this alignment and swing the mirror until the cross is on the airplane. You can use your free hand as a shutter to send S-O-S signals.

A simple but effective heliograph can be made from a bright tin can lid or two mirrors (figure 9-5). Scrape off a small dot of silvering in the center of each mirror to make a "hole", then tape or tie the mirrors together, reflective side out.

SMOKE SIGNALS

Every kid knows how to make smoke signals. Just build a small, brisk fire then throw on green leaves or grass. On a still, high pressure day, the smoke will drift several hundred feet upwards without losing shape. A damp blanket (best)

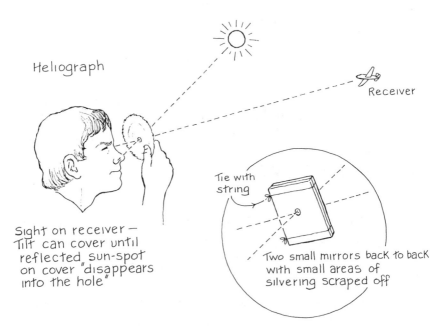

Heliograph

Receiver

Sight on receiver —
Tilt can cover until
reflected sun-spot
on cover "disappears
into the hole"

Tie with string

Two small mirrors back to back
with small areas of
silvering scraped off

Figure 9-5

or canvas pack, used like a camera shutter, interrupts the column of smoke to form signals. Two shutter-like motions of the blanket equals a dot (in the Morse code); six counts is a dash. Use 10 puffs between words. The three most common Indian smoke signals were:

One long column of smoke: "this is our camp".

Two fires and two columns of smoke: "c'mon over to talk".

Three fires and three columns of smoke: "danger or help".

Just about everyone knows these common distress signals:

1. Three successive shots or noises followed by an interval of silence.
2. A gun fired at an interval of one minute.
3. Any national flag flown upside down.
4. Smoky flames from an oil barrel.
5. Morse code transmission of the numeral 9 (dash, dash, dash, dash, dot).
6. The code letters NC.
7. In daylight: a gun shot followed by smoke. At night: a gunshot followed by a red rocket.
8. Rapidly repeated shrill of a whistle or horn.

Other common ground to ground, ground to air, and river rescue signals are illustrated in figure 9-4.

TRAIL SIGNS

There is a magnificent river just west of Lake Nipigon which veteran canoeists speak about with reverence. Along its length is one of the most magnificent waterfalls within the timberline. Here, at "Mink bridge portage", the entire

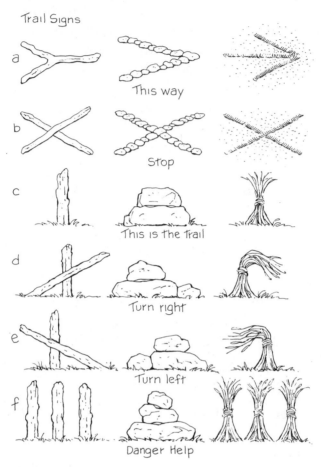

Figure 9-6

contents of the river spill tumultuously downward 250 feet in three successive drops, over a total distance of about a mile, creating one of the most awesome and beautiful white-water areas on the continent.

You can stand at the top of the upper falls and view the stair-step show in its entirety. As one voyageur commented: "It is the land of the lost!" Getting canoes and gear around the lower cascade is interesting: it involves lowering everything by rope 60 feet down a canyon wall.

Mink bridge portage is long overgrown. What remains is a network of animal trails and treacherous shoulder-high boulders. Years ago, some passing canoeists attached a climbing rope to trees at the canyon lip so future voyageurs could bypass the deathly quarter mile boulder hop.

Locating the "safe route" with its attendant "canyon drop" requires a detailed knowledge of trail signs. Well-meaning guides have used every trick in the book to direct the way. Peeled, angled sticks, hard to spot blazes and rock cairns alternately point the way to the dangling rope. The critical left turn (go right and you negotiate the boulder field!) is indicated by a small pile of three rocks—the standard trail sign for the purpose. A heavy rock cross ("stop") defines the location of the first drop.

The person who set out the trail signs must have been an old scout leader, for the "this is the trail", "right turn, left turn", and "stop here" signs are common folklore, right out of the Boy Scout handbook. When I first did the river (whose name I prefer not to divulge) in 1978, there were no trail signs. I searched for an hour for a credible route before I gave up and reluctantly portaged the boulder field. When I returned in 1981, I found the cairns which led right to the rope.

Despite the government's (the U.S. and Canada) willingness to adorn the backcountry with brightly painted aluminum trail markers, natural, U-build 'em trail signs are very much in vogue in wild places. Rock cairns—some of which are centuries old—are still widely evident on the barrenlands. And in the swampy grasslands further south, knotted grasses, crossed sticks, and ever-freshened tree blazes guide the way. For those who go beyond the beaten path, interpreting and building the trail signs illustrated in figure 9-6 remains an essential skill.

ten

• • •

Emergency Camp Gear and Survival Procedures

On August 29, 1911, a 50 year old Yahi Indian, walked reluctantly from the stone age into the light of modern civilization. Tired, hungry and clad in simple native clothes, "Ishi", as he came to be known, carried a bow and stone-tipped arrows he had made himself. A wooden fire-drill, flint knife and leather provision bag comprised most of his worldly possessions.

Within hours after his "capture", Ishi, who spoke only Yahi, his native language, was bathed and dressed in white man's clothes and locked in the Oroville, California town jail where authorities pondered his fate. Three days later, University of California professors T.T. Waterman and A.L. Kroeber laid claim to the stone age Indian as an "anthropological" find and put him to work in the Museum of Anthropology making native tools like the ones he carried when he was apprehended.

A kind and gentle man, Ishi was eager to demonstrate his skills and share his religious beliefs with his new friends. A patient and jovial teacher, Ishi optimistically accepted his fate and enthusiastically helped unravel the mysteries of his culture until he died from tuberculosis in 1916.

Ishi's people once numbered in the hundreds and ranged across the northern half of California. They lived on grasses, seeds, clover, acorns, deer and salmon. As white men moved west with the gold rush, they brought domestic animals which devoured and trompled the grasses, and sluice dams which silted the streams and destroyed the fish. To survive, some Yahis killed the white man's livestock, and in turn were pursued as thieves. Reprisals escalated, and by 1870 only about three dozen Yahis remained. In November, 1908, white men inadvertently stumbled upon the last four Yahis—Ishi, who escaped, his sister and a crippled old man who evidently drowned while trying to get away and an old woman who was too sick to travel. Thirty months later, Ishi, the last of his people, singed off his hair in mourning and prepared himself for death. Then he walked the white man's road into a startling new life.[1]

Survival texts suggest that all you need to know to survive in a wilderness area is contained within their pages. Learn to make the snares, fish traps, brush shelters, spears, bows and fire drills that are illustrated and you'll experience the same confidence and rapport with nature that was once enjoyed by stone age people like the Yahi's.

Don't you believe it! If those who take that advice seriously could ask Ishi, they would learn that "living off" the land became next to impossible after the white man mucked it up with farms, fences, water pollution, drainage projects and other improvements which put profits ahead of the environment. Ishi, a stone age Indian who knew what he was doing, could barely survive in 1916. Today, he would have no chance at all. In our modern, carefully parcelled electronic society, "wilderness survival" simply means attracting the attention of a friendly search party.

[1] You'll find the complete story of Ishi in Theodora Kroeber's book, *Ishi in Two Worlds.* University of California Press, 1961. A moving film, starring Dennis Weaver is also available.

Parachute unseen into the depths of the wildest North American wilderness; stay put, build an obnoxious, smoky fire by day and a crisp bright one by night and help is almost certain to arrive in a matter of days. The human body is a tough machine: it will endure weeks in a hostile environment with little more than water and shelter. If you have fire, water, and protection from the elements you are almost certain to live through the experience. Most of us have so much body fat that food becomes important only after weeks afield. But gathering food or hunting for it (let alone making the tools needed to kill fish and animals) is an energy-consuming process, one which exhausts calories that are better spent keeping warm and signalling for help. Better to conserve your energy so you'll be alive and in good health when you're found.

Nonetheless, there's a certain fascination with survivalist methods that tempts some normally sane individuals to strap on foot long Rambo knives when they go afield. Few will use these swords for more than sharpening sticks and cutting string and cheese, though some adventurers, lured by the miniaturized "survival components" built into the hollow handle, will try their hand at collecting crayfish, water lily tubers and wild onions. Others will attempt to catch fish with the tiny hook and line that's wrapped around the magnesium-coated fire starter, or slash out environmentally destructive debris shelters like the ones shown in survival books.[2]

In his humorous article, "Survive!" which appeared in the March, 92 issue of *Canoe* Magazine, Larry Rice suggests that would-be survivalists may not like what "nature provides". An experienced explorer and outdoor professional who manages the Marshall State Fish and Wildlife Area near Lacon, Illinois, Rice is a contributing editor to *Canoe* and

---

[2]Only idiots and those who are in real trouble build brush shelters and bough beds today. Everyone else who camps out in wild places follows procedures that don't damage the environment.

Backpacker magazines, and the author of *Gathering Paradise: Alaska Wilderness Journeys* (Fulcrum). I think you'll enjoy his realistic approach to "living off the land".

Survive!

by Larry Rice

No food, no drinking water, no knives, no rain gear, no sleeping bags, no tent. Just the clothes we're wearing, life jackets, paddles and the canoe.

Such were the self-imposed parameters my friend Mike Peyton and I set for our 24-hour "Quest for fire," our minimalist ordeal in the nearby forest. Just for fun, we wanted to create a scenario in which all our camping equipment and supplies were lost to the river (or a bear, or whatever), and we had to survive on wits and skills alone.

My usually supportive wife said us high-tech weenies didn't stand a chance.

I knew better. A few months earlier I had attended a week-long tracking and wilderness survival school in New Jersey given by Tom Brown, Jr., author of *The Tracker.* I was guaranteed that after completing the course I would be able to not just survive but to actually enjoy living on what nature provided. Mike hadn't attended the school, but since his savvy in the woods was greater than my own I invited him along. Besides, an adventure is more fun when shared with a friend.

The setting for The Quest was a 5-mile stretch of river in central Illinois. It had been an exceedingly dry summer and the woods were tinder-dry, the river low and turbid. An hour into the trip I was already thirsty, but we had other concerns as evening approached. Tom Brown, you see, teaches that there is a "Sacred Order" to wilderness survival never to be broken: shelter, drinking water, fire and food—listed in order of priority.

Accordingly, well before dark, we pulled the canoe ashore near a steep, wooded bluff that adjoined a grassy meadow. This was where we would construct our shelter: a debris hut, our survival home for the night.

A debris hut, according to Brown, is the only approved shelter in a wilderness survival situation. Structured around a framework of fallen branches and sticks, and layered and stuffed with any light, fluffy, dead vegetation you can find, the debris hut—if built correctly—creates a sleeping chamber that traps and holds heat. (Debris huts have been field tested to 40 below. Happily, the evening lows for this weekend were forecast for the 50's.) After rooting through the underbrush we heaped together a respectable fall-season, free-standing debris hut in about an hour-and-a-half. Simple.

Next came water, or lack of it. The river not only looked unsavory, it probably would have made us violently ill had we tried to drink it. We found a small flow seeping in the forest behind camp, but even it seemed murky and unappealing. Citing prudence, we skipped the Sacred Order for the moment and went on to fire. Mike did his best with a bow-drill fashioned from a sycamore branch, using only a limestone rock as a cutting tool. But after a half-hour of strenuous stroking, all he got was a little smoke and no coals.

On to food. This was easy. While the field near camp was a veritable produce aisle, we settled for munching on a handful of raw white oak acorns for our evening meal. True, we could have foraged for a wilderness salad but we had scarfed down chocolate brownies just before beginning The Quest, and we weren't particularly hungry.

What we really needed was liquid nourishment. Erecting the debris hut had built up a powerful sweat. But we were still without a source of safe drinking water. So I quietly reached into the pocket of my coveralls. "Want one of these?" I said, producing a couple cans of smuggled beer. "It'll help wash down the nuts."

Mike looked at me in astonishment. "I can't believe it. You, of all people. What would Tom Brown think?"

Who cares what Tom Brown would think? It was because of him that that night I'd be crawling into a moldy leaf hut with acorns still stuck in my teeth.

Besides, except for fire, the Sacred Order was now complete.

In case you're still not convinced that pre-planned meals and shelter brought from home beats scrounging a living from the backcountry, here are some "easy" ways (by native standards) to get supper.

ACORN CAKES

Acorns were a staple of the Yahi diet. Like all nuts, they are very nutritious.

Procedure: crack the acorns and remove the nuts. Boil the nuts for an hour or more (pour off the water as it turns yellow) to remove the bitter tannic acid. Then dry the nuts and pound them into a coarse flour. Add water enough to make a thick batter. A dash of salt and sweetener (sugar or honey) will improve the taste. Allow the batter to stand for an hour (or until thick) then pat into cakes and fry in hot oil, or "twist on a stick" and bake before an open fire. Acorn cakes will last a week or more without spoiling.

BOILED CRAYFISH

I've enjoyed boiled crayfish many times on canoe trips. Crawdads are easy to catch, delicious, and simple to prepare. Catch the critters in a simple net made from your shirt or hankerchief.

Procedure: dump the live crawdads into lightly salted boiling water. In a few minutes they'll be lobster red and ready to eat. Peel off the exoskeleton and remove the big longitudinal blood vein. Dip the tiny morsels in melted butter or margarine, if you have it. Mmmmm good!

BOILED MINNOWS

Use your makeshift "net" to catch minnows. Boil them as above and eat them heads and all, or enviscerated like smelt. Don't invite me to join you for this meal.

CATTAIL HEADS, SPROUTS, ROOTS

Every part of the cattail (except the leaves) is edible. In spring, collect the young sprouts close to the rhizomes (connecting, underground roots). Peel and eat the sprouts raw, or boil 'em up like corn on the cob. They taste a bit like cucumbers. In late spring/early summer, cut the yellowish-green flower heads, remove the husks and boil the heads till tender. Later in the season, gather the sunshine yellow, protein-rich pollen and use it as a flour for breads and cakes. Figure 10-1 summarizes the many uses of this versatile plant.

FRIED ANTS AND BEETLES, ANYONE?

At the outset, I should make it perfectly clear that I have never tried, nor do I intend to try this one. Survivalists rate insects high on the eating scale because they are rich in proteins and easy to catch. Recommended method is to set a small grass fire which kills the bugs and cooks them on the spot. You simply collect the fried remains and eat them, less wings, legs and feelers.

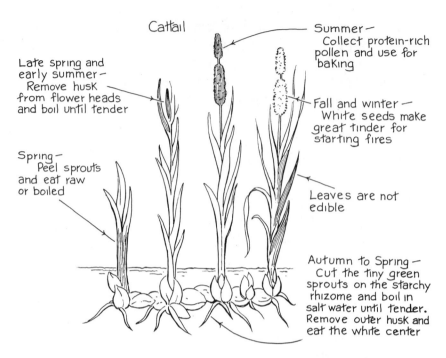

Cattail

Late spring and early summer — Remove husk from flower heads and boil until tender

Spring — Peel sprouts and eat raw or boiled

Summer — Collect protein-rich pollen and use for baking

Fall and winter — White seeds make great tinder for starting fires

Leaves are not edible

Autumn to Spring — Cut the tiny green sprouts on the starchy rhizome and boil in salt water until tender. Remove outer husk and eat the white center

Figure 10-1

Lest you turn up your nose in disgust at this barbaric fare, remember, we're talking "survival" here. Two weeks have passed, your smoke signals and flashing mirror have gone unnoticed, and your belly aches from hunger. Survival experts tell me that at this point even those "of culture and good breeding" will experience a profound change in attitude.

The inner bark and buds of most trees, the stems of dandelions and other greens, and the majority of roots and seeds are edible, if you boil them. Stay away from red-colored berries unless you know what they are (most blue-colored berries are safe), and avoid mushrooms—except Morels, which everyone knows—and plants with milky sap. I've often found large numbers of wild onions growing along the banks of rivers. If you're in dire straits, watch what the animals eat, and indulge accordingly. Change of attitude, remember?

SNARES

Snares, as every trapper will attest, are far more productive than metal traps. Find a runway, suspend a loop of invisible piano wire around a stick (figure 10-2a, b) and you're certain to nab whatever comes by. I've known bird lovers who, at their wits end with squirrels, have set wire snares along the poles which support bird feeders. The snares are illegal, of course—which is of no concern when the issue is surviving a wilderness emergency.[3]

Deadfalls (figure 10-2C) are harder to make than snares but are a good way to catch mice, ground squirrels and foraging birds. Be sure the deadfall is heavy enough to kill the animal.

[3]It is illegal to hunt with any trap, except in a life-threatening emergency.

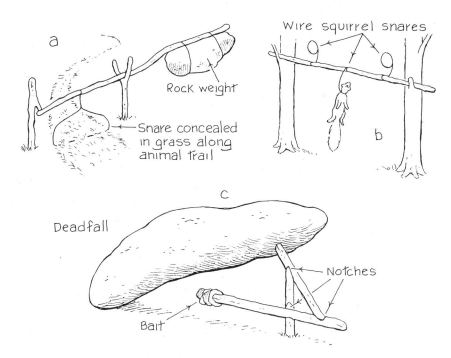

Figure 10-2

FISHING TO SURVIVE

Fishing for food, as everyone knows, is usually far more productive than hunting for it. Large, rough fish like carp and sheephead are easily killed with primitive spears like the ones illustrated in figure 10-3. After a bit of practice, you'll be spearing game fish (it's illegal, except in emergencies) too. In my home state of Minnesota, "spear fishing" is an annual Indian ritual—one which frequently causes friction between native and non-native fishermen. Frogs too, are easily speared with sharp sticks, and their legs (remove all skin: it's poisonous!) make wonderful eating. Best way to spear fish is at night, with a flashlight or torch. The light mesmerizes the fish and makes them an easy target.

If you have a gill net (illegal for sport fishing), simply block off a small stream or set the net between the beach and first drop-off of a lake. In a few hours you'll have lots of tasty fish. Or, construct the simple fish trap illustrated in figure 10-4.

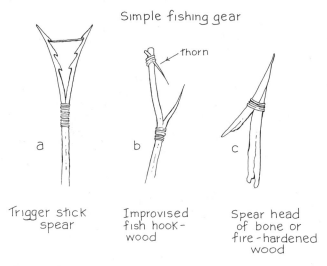

Simple fishing gear

thorn

a

b

c

Trigger stick spear

Improvised fish hook- wood

Spear head of bone or fire-hardened wood

Figure 10-3

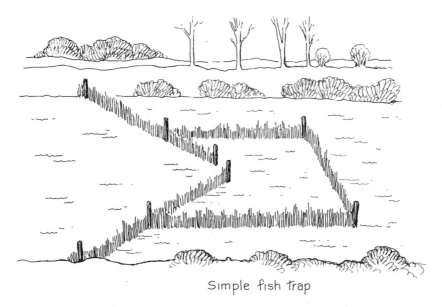

Simple fish trap

Figure 10-4

WATER

When I was a kid, I built a "solar still", per the illustration in a military survival book. I followed the instructions exactly, and I waited. And waited. Nothing. For three days I played with the thing. Ultimately, I got about half a cup of water. Then I read some other survival books and learned that productivity depends upon soil moisture. No soil moisture, no water.

The alternative to a solar still is a "vegetation water still", which is plastic that's suspended tent-like over green vegetation. When the plants transpire in the hot sun, condensed water runs down the "tent" walls. Set a clear plastic ground sheet on the grass in the hot sun and you'll observe this phenomenon.

Getting water by either method requires perseverance, skill and luck. Far better to forgo the sweat of building a solar still and instead seek out more rewarding alternatives.

WATER PURIFICATION

Every camping shop has a variety of water purification chemicals and filters, so I won't waste space detailing them here. However, it is important to remember that certain chemicals are more effective than others under certain conditions. And, treatment with any chemical adversely affects the taste of the water.

For example, iodine kills microbes better than chlorine in cold and cloudy water and, in proper amounts, has no health effects. But iodized water tastes far worse than that which has been treated with chlorine[4] which is a carcinogen. Filtration units, on the other hand, usually impart no bad taste, but are often cumbersome, delicate, and slow to use. And frequent cleaning or filter replacement goes with the territory. There are exceptions, most notably the high speed PUR[5] device, which filters one liter of water per minute and cleans in seconds with a twist of the pump handle.

Boiling is still the most reliable method of purifying water. Some books recommend boiling for 20 minutes or more, which is silliness. Tests have shown that a temperature of 212° Fahrenheit instantly kills everything except the most resistant bacterial spores—which are almost never present in the wilderness—and which can only be destroyed by autoclaving in the laboratory for 15 minutes at 15 pounds of

---

[4]Potable Aqua™ and Globaline™ are popular commercial tablets which release iodine. Halazone™ tablets are the old drug store standby for chlorinating drinking water.

[5]PUR was developed by Recovery Engineering—the same company which received worldwide attention in 1989 when a shipwrecked husband-and-wife sailing team relied on its manually operated desalination pump to survive 66 days in a life raft adrift in the Pacific Ocean. The PUR combines microfiltration with an antimicrobial tri-iodine resin system that kills bacteria and infectious viruses. New for 92 is an easily replaceable carbon filter that absorbs the objectionable iodine aftertaste. Address: Recovery Engineering, Inc., 2229 Edgewood Ave. South, Minneapolis, MN 55426.

pressure. If you simply bring questionable water to the boiling point, you should eliminate all but the most obscure dangers.

Just about everyone has heard of Giardia, the tiny "designer" parasite that inhabits beaver streams. Despite much publicity, Giardia has been around for centuries. Indeed, the highest occurrences are in day care centers where it is transmitted in the stools of babies. Fortunately, most people are enough resistant to the pathogen that problems rarely develop. When they do (after a two week incubation period), the disease is frequently misdiagnosed by big city physicians who have had no experience with it. The drug of choice is Flagyl™, which is available on prescription. Many wilderness travelers routinely carry the stuff.

Though I've guided hundreds of people on canoe trips in the back country, my own experience with Giardia is limited to a single case. A teenage girl contracted the disease while on a canoe trip in the Boundary Waters Canoe Area. Her doctor misdiagnosed the illness and put her on the wrong medication. She continued in misery for a month until her dad casually mentioned her sickness to me. The symptoms sounded like Giardia so I contacted a bush doctor in northern Minnesota for advice. He affirmed the diagnosis and provided proper medication. She was cured in less than two weeks.

TIPS FOR TOLERATING BAD TAP WATER

If you don't like the taste of your city's chlorinated water, try these tricks:

1. Install a copper screen (available at hardware stores) on your faucet. The screen breaks up the water stream and dissipates the chlorine gas into the air.

2. Pour water into a mixing bowl and whip it with an electric mixer. Chlorine gas will be forced out of the whirling water.

Caution: if you have a "final filter" on your drinking water faucet, be sure to clean or replace it at regular intervals. Dirty filters may become over-loaded with bacteria and sediment and may in fact become an incubator for the growth of microorganisms!

3. If your home has lead-soldered pipes, it's almost certain that lead is getting into your drinking water. Symptoms of lead poisoining include lack of vigor, loss of short term memory and inability to concentrate. Simplest remedy is to let the tap run for a few minutes to clear lead particles and accumulated sediment. Do this when you get up each morning and after a long vacation.

By the way, not all bottled water sold in stores is safe to drink. Some brands have been found to contain intestinal bacteria and traces of chloroform. My eighth grade environmental science students have found that some brands of bottled water contain more than 10 parts per million of nitrates, which is the maximum permissible by law. If you buy bottled water, get it from a company whose reputation you trust![6]

FROM THE MOUNTAIN TO THE VALLEY

Scenario: for hours, the treeless ridge has provided easy hiking. Now, it's time to descend the treacherously steep slope to the valley below. You have 120 feet of mountaineering rope.[7] What to do?

---

[6]From WATER WATER, EVERYWHERE, by Cliff Jacobson—an educational unit developed for students in grades 8-12, and published by the HACH Company, P.O. Box 389, Loveland, CO 80539.
[7]Caution: Use only approved mountaineering rope and appropriate slings and hardware for rappelling! Hardware store nylon utility rope is not strong enough for rappelling!

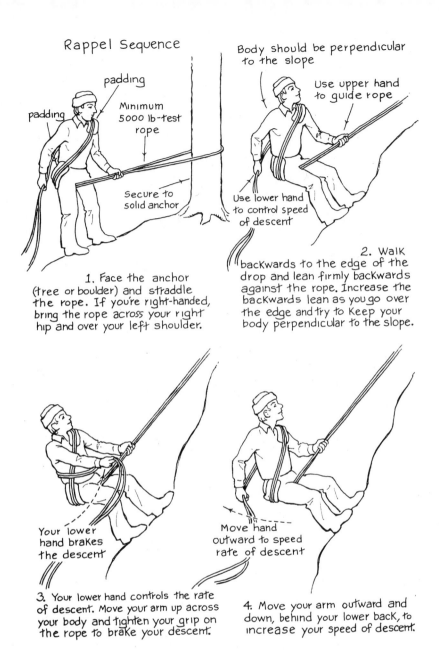

Rappel Sequence

padding
padding
Minimum 5000 lb-test rope
Secure to solid anchor

1. Face the anchor (tree or boulder) and straddle the rope. If you're right-handed, bring the rope across your right hip and over your left shoulder.

Body should be perpendicular to the slope
Use upper hand to guide rope
Use lower hand to control speed of descent

2. Walk backwards to the edge of the drop and lean firmly backwards against the rope. Increase the backwards lean as you go over the edge and try to keep your body perpendicular to the slope.

Your lower hand brakes the descent

3. Your lower hand controls the rate of descent. Move your arm up across your body and tighten your grip on the rope to brake your descent.

Move hand outward to speed rate of descent

4. Move your arm outward and down, behind your lower back, to increase your speed of descent.

Figure 10-5

1. Run the rope around a tree and straddle it, as illustrated in figure 10-5, #1. If you're right handed, bring the rope around your right hip and over your left shoulder. Left handers do the opposite.

2. Lean backward until you feel the rope "take hold" (most beginners don't lean out far enough) and step over the edge of the incline.

3. To brake your descent, swing your right hand forward, across your body and squeeze the rope with your hand. This brings the rope up across your back and creates considerable friction.

4. To reduce rope friction and speed your fall, swing your right hand outward and down, away from your body.

As soon as you reach a secure spot, retrieve the rope (it's doubled, remember?) and secure it around a new anchor.

CHAPTER

eleven

• • •

Bearhavior

It's a familiar scene—the young couple about to embark on their first wilderness canoe trip. On their car is a sleek Kevlar™ cruiser, along with bent-shaft paddles and state-of-the-art gear. The trip has been a year in the planning; no stone was left unturned. Bill and Carly are prepared, in spirit and equipment!

"Goin' for a week," boasts Bill, pointing to the mound of high tech gear on the garage floor. "We'll start at Lake One, swing north to the border, then high-tail it down to Grand Portage. Big carries don't scare us at all: The Kevlar here weighs only 50 pounds."

With that, the pair slip into the padded seats of their sedan and head north to God's country and the great adventure.

Day one begins in luscious sunshine. No wind and not a cloud in the sky. What could be more perfect? In mid-afternoon, Carly spies a high rock outcrop which commands a magnificent view of the lake. It's a popular spot, as evidenced by the tired vegetation and trash-choked fireplace. But no matter: does the realization that others have been here before make the place less beautiful?

"We'll camp here!" says Bill, authoritatively.

As nightfall approaches, the couple looks to the security of their outfit. They've heard bears are about(!), and they have no intention of letting them have their way. First, to locate a "bear-proof" tree.

"Over there," says Carly, pointing to a horizontal pole wedged between two trees. Methodically, Bill attaches a rope to the food pack then lifts it to the base of the pole. Carly ties the rope to a waist-high branch, then recalls that the oil and popcorn was left sitting by the campfire. "No biggie," says Bill. "Just put it under the (overturned) canoe and pile some pots on top (a signal, you understand) so we'll hear the bear if he comes in."

This completed, the two retire to their tent, confident that their food is out of sight and out of reach. They bask secure in the knowledge that they have followed the teaching of camping books and the federal authorities. Their pack and its contents is safe for the night!

Or so they think!

Around two a.m., the racket begins, first with a clanging of pans, then a subtle crack that suggests breaking wood. Minutes later, there's a hollow "thunk," as the food pack falls ungracefully to the ground. Carly and Bill sit bolt upright in the tent, cold white with fear. Ultimately, Bill grabs a whistle and shrieks his head off. The bear hardly looks up.

In twenty minutes it's over, the woods are restored to their former serenity. Flashlight in hand, the couple ventures forth to survey the damage. There, near the fire grate, is the pack—its belly ripped to shreds by the arrow-sharp claws of the black bear. Nearby is the prized Kevlar™ canoe—a broken seat and thwart give testimony to the power of the old sow. Dismally, Bill scans the shoreline with the piercing beam of the quartz-halogen light. Just out of reach floats the aluminum coffee pot—nucleus of the "bear alarm".

The canoe is easily repaired but the pack is not. Worse than that, the food is gone. All of it. What began as a week long trip will finish as a ten hour drive home.

Bill and Carly look wonderingly at one another. They had followed every "bear rule" in the book. Where did they . . . how could they . . . have gone wrong?

This experience is not unique. The scenario is repeated dozens of times each season in state parks and along popular routes in the canoe country of Minnesota, Maine and Canada. What makes it so frustrating is that most of the campers, like Bill and Carly, "followed the rules," which are:

1. Place your food pack in a high tree (at least ten feet off the ground) or suspend it from a horizontal pole set between two trees, or . . .

2. Place food under an overturned canoe. Pile pots on top to function as a night alarm system.

3. Leave tent flaps open so that a bear can walk in and check out the place without resorting to brute force. (This incredibly stupid advice comes from Superior National Forest materials which are distributed to Boundary Waters Canoe Area campers.)

4. Don't leave food in your tents!

Except for number four, the rules are *wrong*. Dead wrong! Let's examine the routine from the bear's perspective.

Bears are creatures of habit. Their behavior is programmed by past experience. They've learned that every canoe party which occupies the site suspends their food pack from the *same* tree. Campers are lazy, thinks the bear. There are other trees in the forest. Why do these idiots always pick the same one?

Even the dumbest bear knows that food comes in packs and packs hang in trees. *Certain* trees! And the bruin becomes very adept at getting it. Consider this incredible scene which I witnessed.

A food pack is suspended in a tree limb about ten feet off the ground, some three feet away from the tree trunk.

Mama bear waddles up, stretches out and begins to climb. She ascends a few feet then slides reluctantly down. She's ticked. Real ticked. So she snaps, woofs and cuts a fuss as she circles the tree, her eyes fixed boldly on the dangling morsel.

Meantime, one of her cubs begins to climb. It gets up about six feet, looks down and bawls. "Mama, mama," it cries! The sow trots over, looks up, then climbs up behind. When she reaches Junior, she stops and nudges his rump. Aptly prodded (on purpose or otherwise), the cub scoots up, stretches out on the limb, and with a swipe of his paw, sends the food pack crashing down. Seconds later, mother and child enjoy a grand meal, courtesy of some campers who "followed the rules."

Consider now the plight of the Kevlar™ canoe. These are camp bears, friends. They're not afraid of man, woman or whistle. Clanging pans just add to the fun. Bears are not stupid, but they've never been taught the "proper procedure" for handling a $1,600 canoe. They might just give the boat a good whap, maybe even bite it in an effort to locate the food beneath. It's tough being gentle when you've got claws and paws. Lucky you got away with a busted seat and thwart. A big strong black bear can probably bite through a Kevlar™ canoe. If not, he'll certainly reduce its value!

Now that we've shown that traditional rules don't work, here are some non-traditional ones that do:

1. *If you put your food in a tree, don't use the same tree as everyone else!* As noted, bears are very adept at getting packs out of trees, even when they are the recommended ten feet off the ground.

   I never tree my packs. Instead, I take them out of the immediate camp area and place them in the woods or along the shoreline. Packs are separated by at least fifty feet for additional security.

   Here's the rationale: Bears know that camps contain food, the reason why they frequent them on a nightly schedule. They also know that the "rewards" come in packs, pack-like objects, and tin cans. Once the animals find these items, they'll tear them apart or scurry off into the woods with the object in tow. However, bears have very poor eyesight; if they can't see the pack or smell its contents, they won't find it. Non-believers should note that bears occasionally rip open tin cans which, as everyone knows, are "hermetically sealed!" There's absolutely no food odor. It's the *shape* of the object that attracts.

Case in point. Some years ago, I served mixed dehydrated fruit to my teenage crew. The fruit had an abundance of prunes, which the kids disliked. So, they responded by throwing the wrinkled fruit at one another. When the fun ended, the area was littered with prunes.

About midnight, a sow and cub wandered into camp and began to lap up the goodies. They came within a dozen feet of our food packs which were stacked just outside the camp perimeter. It was too dark to see, so the bears carelessly passed right on by. Again, let me emphasize that a bear won't get your food if he can't see it or smell it. All of which leads us to Rule Two.

2. *Keep a scrupulously clean camp!* Leftover food should be burned completely or taken way back in the woods and buried. Every rice grain and kernel of corn must be scavanged and disposed of in an ecological manner. Give a bear an appetizer and he'll expect the main meal!

3. *Don't keep food in your tent!* The camping books and feds are right on this one. Bears *will* tear down your tent, maybe maul you to get at the morsels inside.

What to do when a bear comes into camp?

Be cool. The bear is not interested in you. It's your food he wants. I've confronted a number of black bears, and my nonchalant procedure goes something like this: First I yell, maybe blow my whistle. If the bear's wild, he'll hightail it south. A camp bear won't even look up. This being the case, I casually crawl out of my tent to view the show, secure in the knowledge that bruin won't find anything here to his liking. Now—write this in indelible ink on your brain: YOU WILL NOT SCARE OFF A DETERMINED CAMP BEAR! It will only leave once it realizes that there is no food or food odor.

There are exceptions; don't be too laid back. Deskbound environmentalists would have you believe that wild animals will never hurt you, while Rambo survivalists will want to shoot anything that moves. Fact is, there are crazy animals like there are crazy people. In the summer of '87, there was a bad mauling in the B.W.C.A. The bear was sick, underweight and very hungry. She followed the man right out into the lake and kept chomping away while his son tried to fend off the bear with a canoe paddle. Fortunately, the man survived and Forest Service personnel killed the bear a few days later. All of which suggests that you should use caution around these big animals. Take nothing for granted. And don't run! Movement triggers pursuit!

If yelling doesn't solve the problem, it's doubtful more drastic action will. Best look on quietly and let the bear have his way. If the animal confronts you, talk gently and slowly back off. And keep a wary eye for a tree you can climb.

In the unlikely event you are attacked, your best defense is to fight with all your might. *Do not* play dead if you are assaulted by a black bear! For grizzlies, the rule is to assume the fetal position— hands behind neck, body curled tightly into a ball— and be absolutely still. Hopefully the bear will perceive you are no threat and walk away. I can personally attest to the effectiveness of this method.

In 1984, I was "charged" by three grizzlies on the arctic tundra. As they galloped determinedly towards me, I dropped to the ground and played dead, certain the ploy would become fact in a matter of seconds. The bears came within thirty feet, then wheeled off towards the highlands. Later, when I shared my experience with a biologist in Yellowknife, he commended me for quick thinking and "correct" behavior.

4. *Don't put food packs under an overturned canoe.* Bears know all the tricks. And—it's hard on canoes!

These four rules work. Virtually always. But outfoxing bears is easy if you just remember to *take your food packs out of the main camp area before you retire for the night.* Whether you tree them or stack them along the shoreline, per my recommendation, is up to you. The important thing is to break the classical conditioning habit.

Question: If it's that simple, Cliff, why don't other camping writers and the feds support your methods?

Frankly, I'm not sure. I do know that most outdoor writers spend much less time in the woods than they would have you believe. Much of what you read is parroted from outdated camping texts, not from practical experience.

Once, I explained my method to Lynn Rogers, noted North American black bear expert. Lynn listened attentively, then responded, "Makes sense, Cliff. Should work."

It does!

HOW TO DISCOURAGE AN AGGRESSIVE BEAR WITHOUT HURTING IT

It began in 1982 when researchers at Cape Churchill, Manitoba fired 12 gauge "cracker shells" (shells which explode on impact) at problem polar bears to scare them off. This worked fine as long as the bears were more than 120 meters away. Closer than this and the shells often landed *behind* the animal and scared it *towards* the shooter! Moreover, some bears became conditioned to the harmless noise of the firecracker and paid it no heed. And on a few embarrassing occasions, the explosions set the woods afire!

Then, in 1983, researchers at Churchill tried shooting aggressive bears with special plastic "stinger" slugs which were similar to those used by policemen to control riots. To be effective, the slugs had to cause pain, but not injury. This created problems as a projectile that would sting at forty meters, would penetrate hide at ten.

Ultimately, a lightweight, finned plastic projectile with a velocity of 635 feet per second was developed that had an effective range of 60 meters and accuracy enough to hit a water bucket at 50 yards.

As the researchers became more practiced in the use of plastic slugs, they developed a workable strategy: first, they fired cracker shells at ranges of 150-200 meters in an attempt to scare away the bear. If that failed, they shot the bear repeatedly in large muscle groups with plastic slugs at *30-60* meters. Table 1 shows the deterrent-value of the hits. As you can see, results improved dramatically with practice during the second half of the experiment.

Table 1 Deterrent Value of 12 Gauge Plastic Slugs on Bears

Date	Impact in foot pounds of energy	Deterrent attempts/ successful
1982	77	25/0
1983	77	49/27
1984	70	136/107
1984-86	N/A	5/5
1984	N/A	23/23
1985	75	46/46
1986	75	11/11

WHERE TO GET POLYETHYLENE
SLUGS AND CRACKER SHELLS

There are no retail dealers for plastic slugs, but you can get them from AAI Corporation, P.O. Box 126, Hunt Valley, MD21030 (Phone: 301-666-1400). They are dubbed BD-100, or simply "B.E.A.R." , and come packed five to a box at a cost of about $4.00 per shell.

Cracker shells are usually sold in units of five or twenty at around $1.50 each. Most safety supply and wildlife control dealers have them. Caution: be sure to target a few cracker shells before you lob one at a bear. You must know how far they'll travel before exploding. Cracker shells *should not* be fired when the bear is closer than 150 meters or you may overshoot and drive the bear towards you!

THE GUN

Any 12 gauge shotgun with $2\frac{3}{4}$ inch chamber will work, however, your safety requires accurate placement of projectiles. For this reason, a sight-equipped pump-action slug gun (cylinder or rifled bore), with five round capacity, is recommended. Plastic shells don't produce enough recoil to operate the mechanism of auto-loaders, and bolt-actions and double-barrels don't have enough fire-power if you have to fire live ammo in a conflict situation.

If you're trying to discourage a bear with cracker shells and plastic slugs, you should have a friend with a high-powered backup gun standing nearby. If that's not practical, fill the magazine tube with three lead slugs and top off with one or two non-lethal projectiles. This way, you'll have immediate access to deadly slugs if you need them.

Since you cannot afford to have a jam when your life is on the line, gun experts suggest that you modify the pump gun by cutting a long slit in the magazine loading tube. If a shell jams, you can push it forward through the slit.

WHEN PLASTIC SLUGS FAIL

Aggressive bears which are not deterred by cracker shells and plastic slugs may have to be killed—hopefully, in the most humane way possible. Until recently, 00 buckshot was the preferred bear medicine for 12 gauge guns. However, studies have shown that penetration of 00 buckshot into the body of a bear at ranges of 13.5 meters or less, is only about 6 cm over a 30 x 30 cm area. This may not be enough to reach the vital organs of a large bear. For this reason, researchers on the Churchill project emphatically recommend that lead slugs never be fired at a bear which is over 30 meters away.

We choose to travel the wilds of northern Canada and Alaska largely because we will see caribou, muskox, arctic wolf, and the great bears in their natural surroundings. I don't know a single outdoors person who would take pride in killing a bear or other animal on a hiking or canoe trip. On the contrary, a shot fired in self-defense would probably sour the wilderness experience for everyone.

And that's why the deterrent system outlined here should be considered by all who travel among the great bears. Here, in a one gun system, is the opportunity to "educate" a troublesome bear without destroying it.*

*I am indebted to Peter Clarkson, wolf/grizzly biologist, Wildlife Management Department, Department of Renewable Resources, Inuvik, N.W.T., Canada, and AAI Inc. of Cockeysville, Maryland, for their research and recommendations.

Index